# The Vatican Battle of Bishops:
# A View from The Pew

Gil Gadzikowski

BookLocker
Trenton, Georgia

Print ISBN: 978-1-64719-879-4
Ebook ISBN: 978-1-64719-880-0

Published by BookLocker.com, Inc., Trenton, Georgia.

Printed on acid-free paper.

BookLocker.com, Inc.
2023

First Edition

## ECCLESIA SEMPER REFORMANDA

"The Church is always in need of reformation...

In so far as she is an institution of men."

—The Bishops of the Council, Vatican II

# TABLE OF CONTENTS

AUTHOR'S PREFACE...................................................................... 7

PROLOGUE: The Church Before the Synodal Process................... 11

CHAPTER ONE: What's Happening in My Old Church? .............. 23

CHAPTER TWO: What Happened to the Hierarchy? ..................... 29

CHAPTER THREE: What Jesus Said Is Our Mission..................... 39

CHAPTER FOUR: Sources of Reform ............................................ 47

CHAPTER FIVE: Sources of Reform II .......................................... 55

CHAPTER SIX: Sources of Reform III ........................................... 69

CHAPTER SEVEN: The Battlefields ............................................... 79

CHAPTER EIGHT: Why Did Pope Francis Call a Synod?............. 93

CHAPTER NINE: The Parties to the Battle.................................... 103

CHAPTER TEN: The Ultimate Battlefield and Solution
    for the Problems of the Church.................................................. 121

APPENDIX: Is God Just Looking to be a Close Friend?
    Is That Why Jesus Came?........................................................... 145

AUTHOR BIOGRAPHY ................................................................ 159

# AUTHOR'S PREFACE

After Marquette High School in Milwaukee, on August 19, 1949, I entered the Jesuits' St. Stanislaus Seminary at Florissant, Missouri. At the time I presumed I had a vocation to the priesthood, but that wasn't the case. On Christmas Eve, 1957, I closed the door on the Jesuit residence and the Jesuit Order. I remember a gentle Milwaukee snow and my heart full of gratitude to the Jesuits. I am forever in debt to them for their kindness. Most importantly, my spirit was at rest because I had given myself fully to the Jesuit program, although I'd found out I was not called. I'd left the Jesuits, but what I did not leave behind is a deep interest in, and concern for, all things pertaining to the Catholic Church. I had fallen in love with what Church really is: an astounding relationship whereby God and his children talk to one another!

I later became a businessman. During my business career I paid regular attention to news of the Church. I observed incidents in which a restriction was placed on who was allowed to listen and talk with God. I noticed a pattern emerge: only the ordained were allowed to listen and speak to God. I thought this was unfortunate, but now many years later I see hope: Pope Francis is calling the pew-Catholics to tell of their concerns and their inspirations from the Holy Spirit. The Pope is telling the Hierarchy to listen.

Fortunately strong voices, especially German Catholic women, are speaking. Others have joined them. As one might expect, powerful members of the Hierarchy are resisting. There is indeed a skirmish, and Pope Francis is in the middle of the not-so-subtle fighting. He is trying to keep both sides loyal to the Church, but that is becoming more difficult with a slow hardening of positions by each contending faction. In order to have time to address the potential fracture, some observers believe, Pope Francis has postponed the final assembly of the Bishops for the Synodal Process until October 2024.

Either way, Francis has hold of the proverbial tail of a tiger. His postponement of the Assembly of Bishops is his reaction to the build-up of tensions: Francis measured the depth of the resistance of some Bishops and Cardinals; he observed the swarm of serious challenges by the pew-Catholics. He concluded they both needed time to cure. At the same time, certain Bishops and Cardinals consider the Synodal Process a waste of time because the laity are not anointed. Finally, a considerable number of leading pew-Catholics have demonstrated a determination not seen before. The Bishops rely on tradition; the lay-leaders come with accelerated theological developments.

The Pope knows there is no turning back at this point. As most executives know, to stall on a problem can be a very simple and effective tool of management. However, at some point the shuffling of the deck has to end and the cards need to be dealt. Hence, Pope Francis wants time to avoid a public showdown.

Having postponed the Assembly of Bishops, Francis has work to do—to temper the Hierarchy who drown in a culture that says *WE* are the Church; and to cultivate the laity whose impatience demands that *NOW* is their time. How does Francis reconcile the two? Does the Holy Spirit have a solution up its sleeve? There's a battle brewing in the Vatican—this book draws its name from it: the battle is between Bishops, opposing Bishops, and pew-Catholics. They are battling over who owns the Spirit.

**A Special Note to the Reader**

The book does not discuss the Hierarchy's claim to authority based on what are called the "commissioning passages" in the New Testament. You probably can recall them by heart: "Peter, You are the rock…" and "The gates of Hell…" and "Go and teach all nations…" and so on.

These passages have been thoroughly examined by Biblical scholars who have written many books about their validity, pro and con. Therefore, there is no need for an extended discussion here. To state this book's position on those passages and the reasons for that position will suffice.

This book accepts the position of independent scholars who have concluded too many serious questions arise from the text of the "commissioning passages." The problems in regard to the text's history, authorship, idiom, word usage, and purpose have caused independent scholars to conclude the passages to be accretions. In addition to the problems with the texts themselves, serious questions arise that are problems associated with all oral histories.

Also there is one theological dispute, still unresolved, among the theologians and the scriptural scholars. How one interprets the fact of two different Greek names for "Peter" in the same passage makes a difference: does the passage apply solely to Peter as the head of the Apostles, or to Peter as head of the disciples? That leads some scholars to understand the commission in a very broad and extensive sense: Peter is viewed as head of all the disciples (all believers are commissioned) as opposed to Peter as head of the Apostles (only he and successors are commissioned).

Finally, this book accepts the gospels not as history but as four theological treatises. Each is written to show Jesus is God and differing as to when Jesus became God. As to when Jesus became God, Matthew has Jesus become God at his baptism: the heavens part to the voice of God (i.e., "This is my beloved Son"). John has Jesus as God before history: "In the beginning was God and with God." Luke has the Archangel announce Jesus as God at his conception, and that is followed by choirs of angels at Jesus' birth. Mark is concerned about Jesus' Jewish-ness, and his exhaustive "begats" are meant to trace Jesus back to King David, royalty, and to Divinity.

Biblical Scholar Fr. Raymond Brown, OSB, cautions us the evangelists were competing at the time with the Caesars as gods. The various natural miracles attributed to Jesus are the response to the sighting of a comet in association with Caesar upon his death.

Finally, the most practical reason for not including the discussion of the "commissioning passages" here is to keep the book under 200 pages in order to maintain the spirit of brevity.

# PROLOGUE:

## The Church Before the Synodal Process

In an August 2019 letter, Pope Francis urged his priests to consider the sin of the Church's Hierarchy as a call to purification. Pope Francis refers to the condition of the Church as the Spouse of Christ being "a Bride caught in adultery." The admission of sin is very sad because we were taught the gates of Hell shall not prevail against the Church. But we need to remember a little bit of Latin from Vatican II: e*cclesia semper reformanda* translates to, "The Church is always in need of reformation." Vatican II reminded us the Church is an institution of men here on Earth. The leadership of the Church can and did sin, and not just once, as we shall find out as we learn more of what's happening in our Church.

### An "Institution of Men" on Earth Sinned

Indeed, the Catholic Church as an institution has sinned. The worst of the scandals was the sin of the Hierarchy—their attempt to cover up the sin and crimes of priests' destroying the innocence of children. The only justification for talking about the sin of the Church is to remind ourselves that the Church on Earth is a "becoming." That is, the People of God have not yet come to be the Kingdom of God. We strive to Jesus-ify this world just as Jesus did. We strive until the end time when we, the People of God, shall be actualized as the Kingdom of God. Therefore, we need be open to new ways and reforms, if necessary, to come closer to realizing the Kingdom.

## Eschatology: Becoming the Kingdom of God

The process of "becoming" in Church theology refers to the study known as "eschatology." Eschatology offers theological conclusions about the grand finale of the world— when history ends. It is the time of Jesus' second coming and the ultimate realization of the Kingdom of God.

Jesuit theologian Fr. Karl Rahner is reported to have seriously considered Jesus was convinced the Kingdom of God would be realized here on earth. God's Kingdom would occur in mankind's history. Just in case Jesus was not waiting for an end time, the need to explore the best paths for his church would then become a high priority right now and right here.

Cardinal John Henry Newman suggested how we should understand change. According to Newman, "Here below to live is to change, and to be perfect is to have changed often." The Cardinal explained that change is a conversion—an interior transformation. Consider this: we have change all around us. Almost every day, there are new "becomings" in all the facets of life including physics, medicine, communications, space science, etc. The Bishops of Vatican II enjoined us to discern the place of those "becomings." They wanted us to judge their value in the overall scheme of the Kingdom of God. In addition, the Church must be committed to its own "becoming." Unless the Church is open to "becoming," its hope and task to Jesus-ify the world will be frustrated and fail. The People of God will not become the Kingdom of God.

Theologian Fr. Richard McBrien of Notre Dame's Department of Theology offered an explanation of the Vatican II document *Lumen*

*Gentium* (i.e., *Light to the World*). He first noted importantly that *Lumen Gentium* defines the Church as the whole people of God. The Faithful of every rank, the person in the pew to the Pope himself, are given the gifts of the Spirit. These gifts are to be used toward the "becoming" of the People of God.

We are to use the gifts for the "sacramentation" of the Church and the world. We are to be the outward sign of God's operation in this world. Fr. McBrien points out that the person in the pew is required to respond to the gifts of the Holy Spirit. He stressed that responsibility comes with the gifts of the Spirit. Pew-Catholics are required to participate fully in church matters—to help the Church be that outward sign of God on earth. And then Fr. McBrien noted our responsibility is very serious; it includes even criticizing Church leaders when there is sin in the Church. The pew-Catholic may criticize the Hierarchy, if necessary in public, when there is sin in the Church.

Fr. McBrien tied our participation in the Church to eschatology. The Church is both "now" and "not yet." To get to the Kingdom, we work in our present "not yet." Thus, the pew-Catholic must strive to be perfect. As Cardinal Newman observed we must change often; we must be "becoming." Furthermore, the Faithful must participate fully in the Church.

Fr. McBrien stressed his point: the Faithful own their gifts of the Spirit, but with these gifts comes a responsibility. The Faithful are hence required to speak out for change—for "becoming." The Church begins with Jesus in history. The Church is right now. The Church becomes the actual reality of the Kingdom at the end of history. Thus, the Church is not yet. Therefore, the word of the day for all Catholics must be "Becoming" and requires our full participation in the Church!

## The Hierarchy and Change

The Hierarchy of the Catholic Church is overly sensitive to even the slightest suggestion of change. Just say, "Change!" and immediately the Hierarchy puts their dukes up. They are ready to battle to maintain the status quo. What is obvious is the Church needs to "become" but the Hierarchy's motto and slogan is "status quo."

Possibly, the idea of change or reform conjures up thoughts of Martin Luther and the Reformation, yet that is such a long time ago. Further, the Bishops of Vatican II talked about reform—about change—in gentle terms, even calling on the pews to become fully helpful. The *Decree on Ecumenism* reminds us that *ecclesia semper reformanda* (i.e., "The Church is always in need of reformation"). The decree notes that Jesus "summons the church to that continual reformation for which she always has need, insofar as she is an institution of men" here on earth. It is there the Catholic Church allows that its administration is a human "institution of men." Therefore, as human, the Church has erred and even now errs, yes, sins: consider the past and present-day violations of Charity. For example, some called women Satan from the altar steps, practicing misogyny; clerics vilified the very person of a homosexual; a one-person Congregation served as prosecutor, judge and jury to deny a theologian his livelihood.

However circumspect the Church might be about admitting its sin, the Decree on Ecumenism recognizes that the Church is provisional. It is never complete in time. It calls us to strive to "become" God's Sacrament on earth, just as Jesus showed what the true "becoming" means. Therefore, *Lumen Gentium,* in encouraging and prescribing that its members be sensitive to the gifts of the Holy Spirit, also encourages and prescribes they level with church leaders about what's on their minds—just as Jesus did during his lifetime, calling out the Pharisees. And the most important but neglected admonition, the Decree on Ecumenism prescribes that the Hierarchy open their minds to what the Faithful tell them.

## Does the Church Hierarchy Listen to the Spirit?

Three factors explain why the Church Hierarchy does not generally listen to the Holy Spirit as spoken to the pew-Catholic. To begin, the Hierarchy is not open to "becoming." They view the status quo as sacred. This is sad, since clinging to the status quo means God has retired and no longer is present to us. The Hierarchy is communicating to us that God isn't involved anymore. All we now have is the Hierarchy. That compares, for example, to several years ago. There was a "God-is-Dead" movement. The message of the God-is-Dead movement was God no longer cares; we have been left to ourselves; we now need to duke it out among ourselves as best we might all alone! That hurts because the Hierarchy has eliminated hope. How do you spell despair?

Second, the Hierarchy is truly convinced they constitute the Church. The oils of Holy Orders mark the anointed with the special gifts needed to guide and oversee God's society. They have codified their special status in a Church Canon, which indicates only the ordained may govern. Yes, the Bishops often say the right words, words like "People of God," but one wonders, do they mean them? This is a legitimate question because they consider they alone constitute the Church, and there is no reason to listen to the Faithful.

Finally, the Hierarchy has traditionally been a caste of privilege. The privilege came by accident. The Hierarchy took to the privilege almost by osmosis. The Roman Emperor Constantine gave the clerics official Roman rank which in turn commanded honors and status, and very telling, a paycheck to go with the rank. That resulted in the clergy being no longer required to work for a living alongside the regular believers. As a result, they lost touch with all the other believers in Jesus. After enjoying their privileges and pocketing the funds, over time they began to puff themselves up in fancy Church robes and titles. Hence, they eventually became "Your Eminence." Given the privilege, they considered their rank, status, and funds were a result of their ordination, not an accident of history, of Constantine's beneficence. Therefore, in their minds, the class of the ordained are above and beyond listening to the laity.

**Preserving the Status Quo**

The Council on the Amazon confirms how Rome is stuck in the status quo. Pope Francis called the Council on the Amazon to order with great fanfare. Answering his call, there were heavyweight discussions and consultation between Cardinals, Bishops, and laity who worked in the Amazon. Consequently, they developed a multifaceted set of recommendations. In particular, the Bishops of the Amazon recommended the Church ordain priests from among the *probati,* men of the region who are proven and committed to true Jesus values. The Bishops also recommended the ordination of female deaconesses. Those who would be ordained were nuns, and women who were already working in the remote villages of the Amazon. The motivation was to provide for the native Catholics off in the hard-to-reach forests of the Amazon the Mass and the Sacraments more than once a year.

Oddly enough, Pope Francis passed over those recommendations. Francis did not even acknowledge them. In turn, he deliberately ignored change in the Church and concentrated on what businesses should do about trees!

Why the deliberate disregard? The ordinary person has trouble understanding the Pope's mind: Francis emphasized forests and neglected the people! But is Francis not the Pastor of the People? We know he is not the Forest-Ranger of the Trees, but still Francis skips over the Cardinals, Bishops, and lay persons' sincere recommendations to "become." Thus, Pope Francis sticks with the Hierarchy in maintaining a frozen course to foster the "status quo."

**Synodal Church: Communion, Participation and Mission to Open October 2021 and Close October 2023**

Pope Francis has called the Bishops of the world to a Synodal Process. Over two years, the Bishops are called to discern the Holy Spirit as it is expressed through the People of God. The Synodal Process offers the pew-Catholic hope. The pew-Catholic heard Cardinal Mario Grech, Secretary-General of the Synod of Bishops, speak of the need for the sense of the Faithful. He is quoted as saying that "without consultation... there would be no Synodal process." Very to the point!

Nevertheless, Cardinal Grech added a serious reservation by urging a "listening to...the synergy of the People of God...each according to their proper function." There's the rub! Question: what does the Hierarchy see as the Faithful's "proper function?" They consider the Faithful's "proper function" as second class. Is Cardinal Grech promising to listen to the People of God if they speak what the Hierarchy wants to hear? Indeed, that would be deceptive and sad.

What is most sad about the Hierarchy's stance to preserve the status quo is they even deny themselves the excitement of learning something new—the possibility of growing the Church into a more exciting future. They prevent the Church from "becoming" alongside the "becomings" of the world.

**Is the Church the Hierarchy, Not the People of God?**

Pope Francis seems to blow hot and cold. He knows the Church to be the People of God. Sure, he has called for the voices of the pew-Catholics but sometimes he exhibits the Hierarchy's backward attitude. Pope Francis worried about what will happen to the Church after the pandemic shutdown. He recognized the relaxed protocol of the pandemic-Church, the non-attendance at Sunday Mass, the virtual television Masses, the practice of home devotions, even the religious meetings on Zoom. Francis is worried whether they will permanently change the attitudes of the Faithful—and understandably so. Certainly there will be a relaxation and a general casual feeling of freedom. That attitude may very well soften the bond of the Faithful with the formal Church, and Pope Francis is right to fear such an outcome. Nevertheless, it is the way Pope Francis expressed his fear in an April 2020 homily that is strange. He said that people may find a strong spiritual life on their own without the formal Church. People might become comfortable in an intimate isolation with Jesus.

That makes one wonder: why would anyone fear people developing a spiritual life on their own, of getting close to Jesus? growing intimate with Jesus? Pope Francis reveals his reason: "Because people could start living on their own... detached from the Church." In the Pope's mind, the Faithful will be detached from the Church, from the clergy, the Cardinals, the Bishops, and the priests. Only if the Pope thinks the

Church is the Hierarchy can a Catholic be detached from the Church. Pope Francis blows hot and cold—at least at times he seems to express his clericalism. Furthermore, clericalism demands priests mediate between God and the pew-Catholics. The Hierarchy seems afraid to trust God alone with His People. This begs the question: where exactly is the danger in a person's direct relationship with God? Jesus urged us, "The Kingdom of God is within you." The Hierarchy seems concerned that Catholics might go directly to God.

## A Caste of Nobility, Lords over the Masses

In the pews, Catholics have long seen themselves as second-class citizens. How did the Hierarchy arrive at their noble status, the Princes of the Church? The Roman Emperor Constantine initiated the process; seeing the community-minded Christians as a unifier for his empire, he favored the Bishop of Rome with his very own personal headquarters, the Lateran Palace, and made all clergy officials of the State—along with a paycheck!

A paycheck proved to be key. Up to that point, all clergy worked a trade right alongside the Faithful. With the paycheck came release for clergy from having to work. The clergy lost touch and began to think of themselves as above the Faithful. The clergy "became" part of the Roman nobility, were shown deference, and had official power. Over time, while enjoying their regal status, the Hierarchy became convinced their privilege came from being ordained, not a privilege of empire. That's when the clergy took on religious pomp and turned state privilege into Church privilege, thereby the culture of clericalism entered the Church.

## A Frozen, Bureaucratic Catholic Church

Today, the Church Hierarchy justifies itself by its tradition with the motto, "We've always done it this way." Thus, the Church became a frozen organization with frozen operations and frozen doctrines, and worse, frozen minds. The Church today is yesterday-today, and tomorrow is yesterday-tomorrow, etc. "Becoming" is not possible; "becoming" is frozen; and "becoming" certainly would not be allowed because it requires thawing the status quo.

Therefore, the aim in noting the sins of the Church is to focus attention on the very human administrative organization of the Church. The Hierarchy refuses to open up to "becoming," which is essential to fulfilling its eschatological destiny. To freeze the "now" prevents any "not yet." But the Faithful understand the Spirit continues to blow where it will. They are prepared to offer their *sensus fidelium* in the Synodal Process.

## People of God Involvement: Needed Reform

The needed reform of the Catholic Church requires more pew involvement. Talk of reform occasions outrage by the Hierarchy. For example, German Archbishop Woelki of the Cologne diocese has given typical voice to the Hierarchical response to any suggestion that recognizes the pews: "What do they think? The Church is a democracy?"

The response should be, but never is: "Well, as a matter of fact, the Church should be a democracy!" Certainly, Jesus did not have in mind an oligarchic theocracy. In fact, Jesus did oppose the Roman and Jewish theocracies. Finally, a case for democracy in the Church flows rather readily from the decrees of Vatican II, *Gaudium et Spes, Dignitas Humanae,* and *Lumen Gentium.*

This case for democracy is as follows. First, "Joy and Hope" posits the Church in the modern world which is characterized by pluralism. It goes on to exhort each of the Faithful to engage the world as a child of God, steeped in study and devotion. Second, the "Dignity of the Person" emphasizes the gifts of the Spirit are given to each and everyone, the children of God. That makes each vote of a child of God an inspiration of the Holy Spirit. Third, "Light to the World" reaffirms each person's responsibility as a bearer of the Holy Spirit's gifts; an obligation to step forward with their *sensus fidelium.*

Actually, a democratic republic form of governance is a natural way to guide a society that holds a common consensus such as the Catholic Faith. The vote would apply the Spirit's gifts to guide the People of God on their eschatological journey. Thus, there is an answer to Cardinal Woelki's question, "What do they think? The Church is a democracy?"

The answer is this: the Church could be and should be a democracy.

**Conclusion**

There are two problems with the Catholic Church: the Hierarchy think they own the Holy Spirit, and the pew-Catholic is too comfy in his cushioned pew. The Catholic Laity have been enablers of the Hierarchy. The basic and formal difference is how the laity and the Hierarchy view the question: Who owns the Holy Spirit? At times, the Hierarchy have acted against the Spirit and sinned.. Lay folks [some] have challenged the Hierarchy in those instances. In general, the lay folks have had their voices ignored or denied, but The Bishops of Vatican II have decreed and Pope Francis has issued a formal invitation to the pews to present their *sensus fidelium*. Pope Francis has reminded the Cardinals and Bishops that listening is with the heart as well as the ears. This is important since the role of the laity in responding to their gifts of the Spirit presents a serious challenge for the Hierarchy in the Synodal Process. Invited to speak, the pew-Catholics voice their inspirations. The Hierarchy [many] disdain much, if not all, of the Faithful's inspirations. Heavy odds, therefore, suggest a Vatican Battle: Bishops defending the status quo versus Bishops defending the pews.

# CHAPTER ONE:

## What's Happening in My Old Church?

In the letter to his priests, the Pope says the Church is "a Bride caught in adultery." That is very telling because when the Israeli prophets called a sin to be adultery, the Israeli people had fallen into the worship of idols. For example, we have the words of Jeremiah 2:20: "Under every green tree you sprawled and played the whore." Accordingly, Ezekial 23:7 makes the point clearly: "And she defiled herself with all the idols of everyone for whom she lusted." Finally, there's the actual burning of incense to an idol that is tied to adultery in Hosea 1:3: "I will punish her for the festival days of the Baals, when she offered incense to them... and went after her lovers, and forgot me, says the Lord."

Pope Francis asserts the Hierarchy worshipped a false god. They turned their backs on the Holy Spirit. So what idol did the Hierarchy worship? They worshiped their "ordained-only church," a sham church, trying to keep the appearance of "Holy." They were covering up the sins of priests who abused children. They covered up sin to keep "Holy!" Indeed, this is totally warped logic. To stay "Holy" we simply hide sin? Yes, the abuse by priests is also a crime; all the while the Hierarchy was also covering up criminal activity. At any rate, the Israeli prophets would join Pope Francis in calling the Hierarchy adulterers. To top everything, the Hierarchy now pretend nothing happened. The Cardinals, Bishops, and even the Pope act as though it is business as usual. But not every member of the Hierarchy lost perspective.

Germany's Cardinal Reinhard Marx admitted his part in the cover-up of the abusing priests. Cardinal Marx, in a letter of resignation to Pope Francis, confessed his sin. He had allowed the reputation of the Hierarchy to override his concern for the victims in his diocese. The Cardinal admits he turned away from what he knew was wrong. He maintained the false holiness of the priests, bishops, and even cardinals who were involved in abusive behavior and he helped cover up those abusers.

Pope Francis, wisely, did not accept his resignation. Cardinal Marx's reason to resign was to avoid being a stumbling block in reconciling with the Faithful. But that reconciliation will need honest prelates, and Cardinal Marx is certainly an honest one.

At this point we might wonder as Jesus did when only one cured leper came back to thank him, "Where are the other nine?" We might wonder, "Where are the letters of resignation from all the other Cardinals and Bishops and Popes?" They, too, seemed to act against their consciences, snub the Holy Spirit, preserve a false "holiness" for themselves and the abusers. Are the other Cardinals, Bishops, and Popes without consciences?

**The People of God Stepped Forward**

What happened to the People of God when all of this was going on? Did the members in the pews just sit there? The answer is "yes" and "no." Let's examine this: most pew-Catholics sat in their pews and did nothing because most did not know what was really going on. Some were perfunctory in their attendance at Mass, and they didn't know or care. Others heard of the abusive priests but they just could not bring themselves to believe such evil of the priests in their parish. Some heard but had been so gaslighted by the Hierarchy, they concluded it must be a lie from some disgruntled Catholic trying to make trouble for one of the priests. Others were sure such evil could not happen in the Catholic Church.

At the same time, the Holy Spirit managed to alert a few of the pew-Catholics. They followed up on what they had heard. In turn, the Holy Spirit spoke to their consciences: "Trust but verify." When they learned of the abuse, they warned their pastors and Bishops about the problem priests. Their pastors and Bishops went numb, denied, hid the abuse, and some actually dishonored the victims in courts of law. In talking with the parent of an abused boy, hearing of his bootless pleas to the pastor and the bishop, you heard and saw and even felt the insane betrayal of those who pretended to be the "Consecrated Holy." Moved by the horror the victims and the parents faced, Catholics went on to provide comfort, support, friendship, and necessary counseling. Still other pew-Catholics filed lawsuits against the priest or parish or diocese after they were stonewalled. The Holy Spirit guided and provided them the spiritual courage to challenge the pastors and bishops who knew it was terribly wrong, sinful, and even criminal.

As the scandal of the abuse widened, the Holy Spirit did not allow silence to cover the snub the Hierarchy had dealt the Spirit's counsel. An offended Spirit counseled Pope Francis to call for a Synodal Process to allow the pew-Catholics voice. Because the pew-Catholics had listened to the Holy Spirit, the Paraclete now favored them with the spiritual opportunity of a Synod. Thus, the pew-Catholic is given a chance to talk and, hopefully, according to the rules of the process, will be heard by the formal Church.

## An Institution of Men on Earth

The Bishops of Vatican II were wise to remind us that we are in a Church society, "an institution of men on earth." We've seen this evidenced in the cover-up of priest-criminals. Other instances evidence the Church as an institution of men: the baked-in practice of Church misogyny in the very worship of God, the sometimes ferocious denigration of the person of homosexuals, the deliberate and arbitrary censure of dedicated theologian-scholars, and sad and most recent, the Vatican admission of failure not to vet and then to rush the canonization of Pope John Paul II, only to recognize a besmirched sainthood of a prelate who enabled priests to abuse the innocent.

Several Cardinals and Bishops have awakened to the injustice accorded women in the attitude and practices of the Church: the German Bishops meeting in Synod-like with representatives of German Catholics voted 83% "pro" and 15% "con" whether to include women in Holy Orders. Also, Pope Francis has evidenced a more pastoral approach to homosexuals. The Pope has allowed and, in a way, encouraged research on the edge of theology—subject to the final say by the Magisterium, of course. The Vatican has owned up in its report to the failure to vet Pope John Paul II adequately in the process of declaring him a saint. Perhaps, some members of the Hierarchy have begun to appreciate they are indeed an "institution of men."

## Summary and Conclusion

The Church Hierarchy rejected the guidance of the Holy Spirit. They fell into the sinful practice of denying the instances of priestly sexual abuse. When confronted, they moved abusive priests from venue to venue where the abuse continued. The Hierarchy did this with the idea of trying to keep their image as "Holy" before its Catholic membership and the world-public.

The pew-Catholics heard about the abuse of altar boys, usually through the parish grapevine. Some who heard took action. After being stonewalled, the advocates sought recourse in the civil courts where they were met by legal teams of diocesan lawyers. Now comes the Synodal Process, expected to be a confrontation in the Church, but it's the Holy Spirit's home court. The confrontation is of the Holy Spirit's making; it is the inspiration of the pew-Catholic against the Hierarchy's claim to exclusive inspiration by the Spirit. That confrontation could very well result in serious—perhaps ugly—battles. The battle might very well be characterized as the pulpit against the pews.

# CHAPTER TWO:

# What Happened to the Hierarchy?

What happened? Why did the Hierarchy reject their consciences to sin against the Holy Spirit? The explanation is clericalism. Let's define it: Clericalism is the Hierarchy's culture of self-superiority. The Hierarchy is infatuated with the thought they act and speak for God. They consider they do not have to account for their actions. They also give themselves special—perhaps extravagant—titles like "Princes of the Church" and wear robes of royal purple. They expect to be treated with reverence and reject any and all recommendations from the pews.

Clericalism is explained by an accident of history: by way of review, it was the generosity of Emperor Constantine that favored the clergy of the Church with official rank and a paycheck, but the clergy took it as a privilege of their ordination. As a result, this privilege placed them "above" the pew-Catholic. For that reason, they considered that they held full reign in the Church. Even though the benefits obviously came from the Emperor, the clergy forgot and associated their privilege with their ordination. That's why we have a Hierarchy who consider they are above the laity simply because they are ordained; why they consider they are entitled to reverence and a paycheck; why they consider they are to be in charge.

## Accidents of History Influenced the Formation of the Church

How the Church developed a Hierarchy in the first place is an accident of history. We learn from St. Paul about the need for bouncers at the Jesus memorial meal. He reports some folks were into the wine too deeply for their capacity. Over time, one will learn, those bouncers became leaders by assuming more and more authority over the proceedings of the Jesus memorial meal. But first, it is important to know how the early followers of Jesus came to hold a memorial meal.

## The Jesus Memorial Meal

Jesus was a "phenomenon" when he visited villages to teach and comfort and heal. Naturally, he made a very lasting impression. Some villages (and one known as the *Diddache* community) wrote a set of life instructions for their progeny. The rules were based on what Jesus had taught them. Jesus was obviously someone to be remembered. And the villagers did.

In ancient societies, it was common to conduct a memorial meal in honor of the recently deceased. Most of the memorials were styled along the lines of the Roman funereal societies. In Rome, a person not wanting to be forgotten after death joined a funereal society for a fee. That group held a meal in honor and memory of that person upon his death. The Jewish people of the villages visited by Jesus decided to hold meals in honor and memory of Jesus.

At first, the Jesus followers attended their Jewish temple, but were eventually asked to leave. Then, they turned to their homes where the Jesus followers decided to hold their memorial meals. At the start, the leader-presider was the person who organized or sponsored the meal at his or her home. These times came to be known as the period of "home churches." It's likely a round robin of leadership occurred, finally settling at one or two homes after it became apparent what number of people to expect and the size of the home needed to accommodate them. Given a place to hold the memorial meal, the head of the household, say the owner, became the presider over the meal.

St. Paul attests in his letters to a reprimand he gave certain followers of Jesus. They were taking advantage of the sponsored food and drink. They would show up early or would push ahead of others to beat the other folks to the goodies of the potluck. That certainly violated the spirit of the Jesus memorial meal, and Paul wrote to his disciples to correct that. Another of Paul's reprimands was directed against those who became intoxicated during the Jesus memorial. Someone was required to deal with those who snuck in early and who imbibed the wine past their capacity. Good order called for bouncers at the Jesus memorial. Hence, this would assure all attendees followed good order.

**Accident of History Number One**

Those bouncers became an entrenched leadership group. They used the initial need for their services to expand to the overall conduct of the meal. They extended their authority and took on the responsibility to define what is legitimate and what is not. They defined the memorial meal that was eventually to become the Sunday Mass of today. This leadership group, as time went on, continued to presume authority and expand control over the operation of the Jesus community. Hence, an accident of history—poor behavior and too much imbibing at the memorial—explains how the bouncers became the precursors of today's Priests and Bishops. It all started with an accident of history: a couple of misbehaving followers of Jesus.

One important note: an accident is not a mandate. The leadership of the Church today does not have a divine mandate from God. They were bouncers who took over the meal. What happens by accident can be changed. The Hierarchy's recent scandalous mis-leadership is a definite reason for reforming the Hierarchy. And for reforming the administration of the Church.

The combination of the need for bouncers and Emperor Constantine's favor on the clergy, both accidents of history, explains how "clericalism" fully developed in the Church. The leaders arrived at a mental state of attitudes, behaviors, and presuppositions causing the ordained to consider themselves worthy well beyond the non-ordained; thereby, the non-ordained became excluded from the Church governance.

## Roman Empire, Second Accident of History

The clergy found the Roman Empire suited them in more ways than rank, status, and paycheck. After Emperor Constantine set the stage for clericalism, the Hierarchy surveyed the operation of the imperial government. How the empire organized and oversaw the people, both their citizens and the non-citizens, appealed to the Hierarchy. The centralization of power would both dovetail with their presumption of power but also reserve the decision making to the incumbents. Besides, the Bishop of Rome had two advantages: he already had an established headquarters, the Lateran Palace, associated with the centralization of secular power. He had access to wealth, spun off from the secular power of the Empire, to finance inchoate and struggling churches outside of Rome; he sought to "buy" their fidelity to his Rome diocese.

What happened occurred quite naturally—very human. The Hierarch went on to incorporate Roman structure, status, and privilege into the Church: no longer needing to hide for fear of persecution, the Hierarchy fashioned an elaborate celebration of the Mass. Magnificent vestments began to adorn the Hierarchy as symbols of power. They puffed up their honor by taking on imperial titles like "Your Eminence." Then, the Hierarchy codified their honorable status above the non-ordained and their sole and exclusive relationship with the Holy Spirit into the laws of the Church—the Canon Law that governs today. Finally, what is clear is accidents of history account for both the existence of the Hierarchy and their clerical culture. Furthermore, none of these accidents of history qualify as a divine commission as the Hierarchy would have the Pews understand.

## The Council of Constance: Three Popes and *Sacrosancta*

At one time in its history, the Catholic Church ended up with three popes because various members of the Hierarchy were too closely aligned with different political national entities. Therefore, the job of a Council of Bishops was to discern who the Holy Spirit intended to designate as truly to be Pope. There were other goals, but to decide a pope was the main reason for the Bishops to meet. The collateral reason was to reform the Church Hierarchy, if for no other reason than because it was embroiled in a dispute over three popes.

The Bishops did their job: they discerned who should be Pope. But the real reason the Bishops had to meet was the failure of the Church Hierarchy to listen to the Holy Spirit in the election of the pope. The Hierarchy listened instead to three different European national interests and ended up being divided over who is pope. Failure to listen to the Holy Spirit caused the disarray in the Church—the process of discernment thrown to the wind. The Council of Constance corrected the Hierarchy's failure by introducing the *sensus fidelium* into the discussion relative to the authority of the Pope and the Hierarchy in general. The *sensus fidelium* is the inspiration and whisperings of the Holy Spirit to the Church at large.

## The *Sacrosancta* Decree

The major footprint of the Bishops in the Council was its decree referred to as *Sacrosancta*. They declared the Pope as subordinate to the Bishops in Council. This decree is considered the height of the discernment of the Council. The Bishops had come to Constance from many lands. They saw within their gathering of the Council a true "Catholicity," but the meaning of "Catholicity" in this context is not only and more than the idea of spatial, global coverage. The "Catholicity" they understood points to a universal consensus among them: the *sensus fidelium*— the Spirit's inspiration of the Faithful witnessed before the world.

The Bishops understood why they were in Council. These Bishops were called on to discern the Holy Spirit. The formal Church organization had obviously dishonored the Spirit; they created the absurdity of three popes! The mission of the Bishops was to bring back the universal, catholic whisperings of the Holy Spirit into the operations of the Church.

The work of the Council of Constance was special: it refocused the Hierarchy's thinking on the Holy Spirit. The Council reintroduced the Holy Spirit's guidance of the Church as the (Bishops') *sensus fidelium.* And as important, the Council gave definition to what "Catholic" really means—the "sense of the Faithful" is not spatial but it is the evidence of the Holy Spirit's guidance among the People of God. Accordingly, the Bishops might very well have quoted Cyprian of Carthage: "I have made it a rule since the beginning of my episcopate to make no decision merely on the strength of my own personal opinion without consulting you [the priests and deacons] and without the approbation of the people."

Rounding out the report on the Council of Constance, a selection from the decree of the Bishops reads: "[The Council] lawfully assembled in the Holy Spirit has its power immediately from Christ... the Papal dignity itself is bound to obey it in all those things which pertain to the Faith and the ending of said schism, and to the general reformation of the Church of God."

## Infallibility and the *Sacrosancta* and *Hubris*

As a reaction to the *Sacrosancta* and the limits it placed on Papal power, succeeding popes followed the usual strategy to handle what is not acceptable: they simply ignored the work of the Council. But Pope Pius IX was not to be cowed by any Council. Pius IX decided to publish an encyclical, *Ineffabilis Deus* (*The Ineffable God*) on the feast of Mary, December 8th, 1854. He declared Mary's Immaculate Conception as a doctrine of the Church under the auspice of infallibility. The idea of claiming to have a power that assures the veracity of what the Pope decrees when speaking officially and formally as a successor to St. Peter was openly supported by the Cardinals. At the same time, there was a serious concern about the claim to be infallible. Among the influential prelates troubled by Pius' announcement was notably British Cardinal John Henry Newman. Newman's expertise was revealed in his theological treatise, *The Development of Christian Doctrine*. Cardinal Newman published his treatise after the Pius IX encyclical. Newman's thesis was that doctrine developed; doctrine was not simply declared; it was obvious Cardinal Newman was troubled by the infallibility issue.

Why Pope Pius IX decided the authority of the Pope needed to be firmly and officially established had to do with the "becomings" in the sciences at the time. The Nineteenth Century witnessed remarkable scientific progress, evidenced foremost by Charles Darwin's *Origin of the Species*. Upon publication the treatise was viewed by many as a challenge to the Church. A featured debate topic was the question of evolution versus creation. Other scientific discoveries were hailed: *The Table of Elements* was published; John Dalton began academic discussion of atomic theory; astronomers discovered Neptune; Edison created a workable electric bulb; and the general adoption of the telephone, radio, and use of electric power came on the scene. Pope Pius IX, concerned about the Church being abandoned and left behind, called for a Council of Bishops, known as Vatican I (1869-1870), to define how the Church was to remain relevant.

Pope Pius IX took an aggressive stance. His consulting theologians developed the schema whereby the Pope may be considered infallible when ruling *ex cathedra*, i.e., speaking officially and calling attention to his role as the successor of Peter. The Bishops of the Council Vatican I voted the Pope infallible. However, the Council was short-lived. With the start of the Franco-Austrian War in 1859, many Bishops hurried back to their dioceses. Thus, fewer Bishops remained than constitute what would be considered a Council. But Vatican I, meeting before the start of the war, lasted long enough for the Bishops to vote and decree infallibility as the authority of the Pope.

Indeed, the Pope, the Vatican Office, and the Hierarchy all now saw themselves as somehow participants in the infallible attribute. They all seemed to embrace the doctrine of the Pope as the successor of Peter. They became enamored with the power implied by the Pope's being in the place of Peter, and by extension, in the place of Jesus and by still another extension in the place of God. Both in formal and informal matters, the Hierarchy used play on words to imply what they offered was somehow an offshoot of Vatican infallibility. They easily fell into a way of thinking because they were members of "the team." That is, they were in a position to speak for God. The Hierarchy began to identify themselves, not explicitly, but slowly and definitely with God. That distanced them from the unordained still further. Clericalism was strengthened: the thoughts, actions, and attitudes of the Hierarchy resulted in a disdain for any opinion expressed by the unordained. The Hierarchy slowly crept into the sin of *hubris*.

Ancient Greeks portrayed in their tragedies what they considered the ultimate sin, *hubris*. Their tragedies acted out *hubris*: tragic characters in their plays always possessed a great gift that led them into an overriding pride, a pride so deep the characters considered themselves to be gods. *Hubris* is the Classical Greek sin of pride-out-of-control; it comes with such arrogance that a person feels no need to account for oneself and considers oneself as not accountable—not even accountable to the gods!

Some indulgence might be granted the Hierarchy. Even in Scripture, the culture and structure of governance is that of a King. Monarchy is the only biblical analogy the Hierarchy has with which to form its culture and structure. Even Thomas Aquinas favored the efficiency of a beneficent monarchy. The question to ask him today, however, is how efficient or how beneficent would Aquinas judge the present Monarchy of the Church.

Another possible reason why the Hierarchy came to a pattern of clericalism is the general primitive condition of early followers of Jesus. Most were illiterate, uneducated, and not in a position to receive refined spiritual nourishment. Working from dawn to sunset, the laborer is not ready for a talk on anything mystical—the spirituality of one's identification with God. Spiritual pablum was about all that the early believers could digest.

For some, even rote memorization of the prayers may have been a challenge. The early Church was a mixed group of Jesus followers with a majority of farm workers, miners, dock hands, laborers up at first light and exhausted after supper. The exceptions were well-positioned widows, tradesmen, and merchants. The clergy was responsible for the instruction of simple people, burdened by hard labor, most trying to survive. This may have led to a poor and stereotypical opinion of the pew-Catholic.

## Conclusion

The Hierarchy does not have a mandate to exercise control of the Church. They arose in the Church and gained power out of accidents of history. The favoritism shown by Emperor Constantine resulted in their culture of clericalism. The Hierarchy's behavior of treating the pew-Catholic as generally ignorant of anything spiritual persists right up to today. They need to adjust their mindsets and recognize the pew-Catholic's new status both as a more sophisticated person and as a child of God as outlined by the Bishops in Council Vatican II. On the flip side of the coin, the pew-Catholic has to accept the responsibility of self-development as a child of God, with gifts to be cultivated and glory to be given to the Benefactor.

# CHAPTER THREE:

# What Jesus Said Is Our Mission

Unless we know where we are going, we are going nowhere. Therefore, to find what's best for the Church, we need to know and understand what Jesus said is our mission. Only then may we conclude what is the best way to organize and operate to get the job done. There is no mystery in this approach; to pound a nail, reach for the hammer.

## What We Know of What Jesus Wanted

Jesus taught and inspired us two ways: by his life and by his teachings. As to his life, he spent all of his days among the outcasts of the Jewish community. He was known to violate the taboos of his society. His enemies, in their hate, accused him of associating with tax collectors and women of ill repute. Indeed, Jesus emphasized the worth of each person by his friendship among even the least-regarded class of society; we learn from Jesus everyone carries the dignity of a child of God.

Jesus declared each person's worth another way: he ate with whoever happened to be at the meal. Scholars call that pattern of dining *commensality* (from the Latin for "with" and "table," which means "eating together"). For the Jews, not only with whom you associated was important—with whom you ate told the world about you. Jesus' practice of commensality—he ate with whoever was there—shows he regarded everyone as valued equally. His enemies tried to belittle him: "He eats with sinners." But their accusation simply proves Jesus' point: everyone is valued by God.

The Jewish code of honor also prescribed seating arrangements at a dinner. The head table held the most-honored persons there. The honor of other guests was measured by the distance of their table from the head. Recall Jesus' advice, "Take a lower table, then when the host tells you to go to a higher table, you will have been honored." Again, Jesus ate uncaringly about where he and others sat; he enjoyed whoever was his present human company. All are equal in Jesus' eyes.

## Conclusion

The conclusion is obvious: by his way of living, Jesus taught everyone is equal in God's eyes. There's no difference between the rich or the poor, Jew or Samaritan. In Israel, Jesus paid attention to the poor. In general, he focused on the "little" people; he occupied himself with the plain folk. Jesus lived bald equality; scholars call it "radical equality."

From Jesus we learn the People of God are all children of God with the same birthrights. But what of the problem of the Church and the Hierarchy's decision they are superior to the pew-Catholic? The question is whether one considers that ordination brings greater importance to the cleric. In fact, Jesus said, "I've come to serve, not to be served." Ordination designates the cleric as *servus servorum,* the servant of the servants. That is the very motto in the Papal Office itself.

## Jesus Taught Us in Parables

Jesus taught by simple stories folks could remember and think about later at their leisure. In Jesus' parables, there are symbolic indicators of what Jesus intended for his followers. Therefore, many of the stories were shocking to Jesus' audience. Some parables sent the Jews home having to wrestle with the story just to understand it. Scholars have linked together Jesus' parables to provide an insight into Jesus' message telling us what our mission is.

The research of Professor Bernard Brandon Scott, Professor Emeritus, Philips Theological Seminary, demonstrates the mission Jesus gave us. Professor Scott linked together three of Jesus' parables to show what Jesus intends as our Church mission. He starts with the parable of the unleavened bread, then goes on to the parables of the broken jar of meal, and then the Samaritan—the rescuer. Taken together, Jesus tells us how we are to build the Kingdom of God; what to expect as we work for the Kingdom of God and what not to expect. Jesus geared us up for our mission with these parables. Let's look at them more closely.

## Parable of the Unleavened Bread

The background to the parable is that unleavened bread (flat bread, free of yeast) is the bread the Jews customarily ate. Jesus tells the parable of the unleavened bread: "The Kingdom of God is like a woman who when making her bread adds a portion of leaven (yeast) into her mix." That shocked the Jews. Who would do that? The Jews did not bake the bread with yeast because they considered yeast unclean. The Jewish audience couldn't believe what Jesus was saying: the Kingdom of God contains the "*unclean!*"

Jesus used irony to get the attention of his audience, and he did so to have them think about what he was telling them. Therefore, Jesus knew his audience would wonder about something unclean being mixed in with bread that represents the Kingdom of God. Something unclean in God's place? So they asked themselves: where do we experience a mix of what's holy with the un-holy? Well, they likely remembered the verse: "The sun rises to shine on the good and the bad." That answered their question. Right here, right now, in our everyday lives we experience good and bad people and events. They conclude Jesus says the Kingdom of God is here, in our town, and on our street, and in our home. We work and build the Kingdom of God right here in our world with a mix of good and bad. In a sense, Jesus is warning us that while working to build God's Kingdom, we will experience the unholy at times; don't be surprised.

**Parable of the Jar Leaking Meal**

In the parable, a housewife carries home a broken jar with the family meal. Jesus doesn't say why the housewife does not notice the jar is broken. He simply says she purchased the family meal, placed it in a jar, and when the woman arrives home, she finds the jar empty of the meal! Either way, we know the jar is empty and broken; in turn, the meal leaked out. What is Jesus' point? This is Jesus' description of the Kingdom? The housewife and her family go without supper, suffering the consequences of a broken jar? Most likely the Jews had to scratch their heads. Broken jar means leaked meal. Leaked meal means no supper. Maybe they then put together cause and effect. Jesus tells us that even in the Kingdom of God, cause and effect operate. Why would Jesus make a point like that? Jesus wanted to stress that even in God-stuff, the way things work is the way things work. You need to take into account the cause and effect. Or, looked at from God's point of view, "Do not expect a miracle! I'm going to respect how I set the world to run. Besides, I'm not going to do your work for you."

Jesus obviously is talking about our unclean world because things break. He reminds us that things work the way God made them to work; therefore, keep cause and effect in mind. Some folks like to tell the story that gives perspective to prayer; they tell of how the monks prayed for electricity after their lights went out, but nothing happened until one of the brothers went down to the basement to flip the circuit breaker.

**Parable of the Good Samaritan**

To understand and appreciate the Samaritan parable, we must know a real rivalry and suspicion existed between the Jews and Samaritans. The reason was they vied with one another for what was left of the crops and produce after the Romans satisfied themselves. They were engaged in what's called a zero-sum game: the pot is fixed. With two players, if player A gets more than half, player B must necessarily get less than half. In the case of the Jews and Samaritans, there was only so much left over from the Romans (the fixed pot). The Jews worried if the Samaritans got more than half, then they would get less than half. And vice versa. Jesus plays on that rivalry and suspicion to drive home his point in the parable.

The parable is as follows: a Jewish traveler falls into the hands of a highway robber who injures his victim badly enough that the victim is helpless at the side of the road. Several Jews of various rank travel that route, but upon seeing the victim in the ditch, they turn their eyes away and walk on past. Now comes a Samaritan; he sees the robbery victim lying hurt in the roadside ditch; it's a Jew but he sees the need for help and helps him, bandaging him up right then and there as best he could. Then, the Samaritan carries the victim on his own burrow to the Town Inn; the Samaritan arranges with the Inn Keeper for the continuing care of the Jewish victim at the Samaritan's own expense. Jesus' Jewish audience would certainly get their attention grabbed by this one. In Jesus' time, that would be a front page headline in the Jerusalem New York Times: "Samaritan Saves Jew."

Why was Jesus teasing the Jews? Jesus tells his fellow Israelites what is obvious: it doesn't matter who does a merciful action when needed. It was embarrassing the victim's own clan passed him by; a known rival rescued the victim. Jesus makes the rival the hero; the Samaritan gives his time and treasure for the care of the Jewish victim. The Jewish audience of Jesus was sure to remember Jesus' lesson.

The lesson Jesus is offering is powerful: if someone needs help, if something good has to be done, if there is need to love or show mercy, it doesn't matter who helps out! Compassion and mercy have no ethnicity, so even if you don't like them, help them out. Help everyone—even your rival. Set no ethnic limit; in fact, set no limits! Allow everyone to spread goodness. Get the Kingdom going. Jesus is pushing the notion that when it comes to good works, don't let any prejudice, misconception, or rivalry get in the way.

The scholars summarized these three parables in this way: the Kingdom of Heaven is here, right in this mixed up, unclean world of ours. Don't sit around on your hands waiting for God to take care of things; God is not going to do your work. Use your head and your hands and get to work with the help of anyone who will work for the Kingdom. No one is excluded from the work; all are welcome.

Buried in Church theology is a confirmation of our Jesus-assigned mission; it is called eschatological theology. Recall that eschatology is the body of theological understandings about the grand finale of the world. In eschatology, the Church recognizes the limited and unclean condition of the People of God. The People of God are limited in time and space, but they become ultimately the People of God at the end of time. Remember, even Jesus was limited in space and time, Israel, and his century. Those limitations gave rise to Jesus' need for a People of

God to spread his influence both in time, over history, and in space, across the globe. The pew-Catholic works to realize the Kingdom of God, engaged in a "becoming" for the Grand Finale. Also, recall The People of God are "now" and "not yet." The Church is as of right now in an unclean world; and not yet in the fullness of the Kingdom. Eschatology, in pointing to the ultimate realization of the Kingdom, confirms the mission of the People of God is immediately here and now in our unclean world.

## Conclusion

From Jesus' life we learn the scope of the Church's mission: everyone is eligible for the Kingdom of God. Jesus practiced radical equality. He didn't break taboos; he fractured them—that applies especially to his acceptance of all as his associates and buddies. All are equal in God's eyes. Furthermore, Jesus told us "The Kingdom of God is within you." Having told us this, Jesus then directs us to spread the Kingdom in this mixed, clean and unclean, world in which we live. Jesus cautions we'll have to work at it; expect no miracles. Finally, enlist whomever you can to help; get as many shoulders to the wheel as possible.

# CHAPTER FOUR:

## Sources of Reform

This and the following chapters survey what tools of reform have actually worked successfully without precipitating a schism in the Catholic Church. Also considered are circumstances that have contributed to effective reform.

### Counsel of Bishops

The most important tool in Church reform is the Council of Bishops. Canon Law now restricts the calling of a council to the Pope or a cadre of bishops. In the past, Emperor Constantine called for the Council of Nicaea and Emperor Marcian called for the Council of Ephesus, but those days are over. The Pope might be cajoled into calling a Council by trusted advisors, friends, or influential prelates in the Vatican. Lay persons who would seek reform in the Church by way of a council must either wait for the Pope to call one or somehow persuade the Pope.

Fortunately for many pew-Catholics with a current grievance or a suggested reform, Pope Francis called for a Synod, but in an unusual and special way. Francis created a new system for registering the agenda items and it involves the laity. Each Bishop is to set up meetings with his people of the diocese to listen to what they have to say. From those comments offered by the people, the eventual agenda will be set for the Assembly of Bishops in Council. Pope Francis has given the pews a chance to put their oars in the water. Consequently, the Councils of Bishops are significant in Church affairs because they present a "catholic" view, where "catholic" is not simply geographic but rather and more importantly the *sensus fidelium*, the Holy Spirit's inspiration of the Faithful across the globe. The bishops hear what's in the hearts and on the minds of the pew-Catholics who listened to the Spirit.

The Council of Constance was self-conscious about their duty to represent the *sensus fidelium.* When the Council of Bishops decreed the *Sacrosancta,* they posited a limit on the Pope's authority, thereby subjecting it to the direction of the Bishops in Council. They ruled in effect that the Pope drives the bus, but the Bishops in Council decide the route. That decree has been ignored by successive popes but never has been rescinded. The *Sacrosancta* is an example of how sweeping the decrees of a Council of Bishops may be. A Council is certainly in a position to offer a new development that bears on a current controversial issue. Hence, there are two Councils of Bishops that appear most fitting to be considered applicable to the current Church situation: the Council of Constance and the Council of Vatican II.

## The Council of Constance (1414 –1418): Regaining the Holy Spirit

As previously noted, the Catholic Church ended up with three popes because various members of the Hierarchy were too closely aligned with different political national entities. Therefore, the job of the Council of Bishops, called to assemble in Germany's then largest city of Constance, was to discern and regain the Holy Spirit and name whom the Paraclete intended to be Pope.

The official aims of the Council were threefold: 1) To resolve the schism of the Church embroiled in a dispute among three parties of the Hierarchy, each claiming their candidate as the designated true pope; 2) To address certain errors of Faith and especially those proposed by John Hus; and 3) To reform the Church Hierarchy (if for no other reason than because it was embroiled in a dispute over three popes).

The Council accomplished an end to the schism by designating Cardinal Otto Colonna (who took the name Martin V) as Pope. The Bishops addressed "tyrannicide", which was an issue at the time in France, and condemned it. The Council worked out a reduction in Papal taxation; they curtailed the Papal power to appoint ecclesiastics in local dioceses, and then decreed simony to be a de facto sin with automatic excommunication. Their declaration of John Hus as a heretic had a sad result; an out-of-control mob burned John Hus at the stake that very night.

Let's review just a bit: the major decree of the Bishops with the greatest potential impact was the decree referred to as *Sacrosancta*. They declared the Pope as subordinate to the Bishops in Council. This decree is considered the height of the discernment of the Council. The Bishops had come to Constance from many lands. They saw within their gathering of the Council a true "catholicity." The meaning of catholicity in this context is more than the idea of spatial, global coverage. Catholicity, here, points to the Spirit's inspiration of the Bishops, a universal *sensus fidelium*. That gives power to the *Sacrosancta* decree because the Bishops were being called upon to discern the Holy Spirit. The formal Church organization had obviously ignored or dishonored the Spirit; they splintered the Church into the absurdity of three popes.

What is special about the Council of Constance is twofold: first, it temporarily re-focused the Vatican thinking on the Holy Spirit, the work of the Spirit as the *sensus fidelium*; the guidance that is to be incorporated in the decision-making process of the formal organization. Second, it gave definition to what "Catholic" really means: the *sensus fidelium* is not spatial, not a geographic-based concept; it is the evidence of the Holy Spirit's guidance to the entire Church. The emphasis was on the Holy Spirit's operating outside of the confines of the Papal Offices.

To round out the report on the Council of Constance, a selection from the decree of the Bishops reads: "[The Council] lawfully assembled in the Holy Spirit has its power immediately from Christ... the Papal dignity itself is bound to obey it in all those things which pertain to the Faith and the ending of said schism, and to the general reformation of the Church of God." The Bishops might very well have quoted Cyprian of Carthage: "I have made it a rule since the beginning of my episcopate to make no decision merely on the strength of my own personal opinion without consulting you [the priests and deacons] and without the approbation of the people."

The Council of Constance and its decree offer an understanding of why and how full participation of the pew-Catholic might be accomplished. If the formal organization of the Church subscribed to the principle that the Holy Spirit resides in the *sensus fidelium,* the true status and true dignity of the pew-Catholic would be incorporated into Church governance. Another important effect of the recognition of the *sensus fidelium* is that it counters one aspect of clericalism, the Hierarchy's presumed exclusive hold on the Holy Spirit.

The validity of *Sacrosancta* has been debated. Definitely the Popes have simply ignored the Council's decree, the usual technique a pope uses to treat a decree with which he disagrees. This practice of ignoring the Council was also employed by Popes John Paul II and Benedict XVI to enforce their disagreement with the decrees of Vatican II.

Villanova University Professor of Theology, Massimo Faggioli, in a NCR article pointed to the tension between Popes and General

Councils on the occasion of Pope Francis' call of the bishops to the Synodal Process. He notes that the tension is in the role of the Pope: is he a front man for the missionary work of the Church as determined by the Bishops in Council? Or is he the ultimate referee over the discernments of the Bishops in Council? The Council of Constance asserted that the Pope abides by the discernment of the Councils. But the *Sacrosancta* has been ignored. However, it has never been rescinded or condemned.

## The Principle of Default Discernment of the Spirit

The occasion for holding a Council of Constance was an obvious failure of the Hierarchy to heed the Holy Spirit; the failure could not be hidden; there were three popes. The Council of Bishops' work was to check with the Holy Spirit and correct the Hierarchy's failure to listen to the Spirit. Furthermore, any failure of the Hierarchy to heed the workings of the Holy Spirit argues for intervention. The People of God, respecting their own lights, are expected to intervene. The People of God (alone or represented by Bishops in Council) bring forward their *sensus fidelium*. Their intervention is based on the principle of "Default Discernment of the Spirit:" If the Hierarchy has not, is not, or will not attend to true discernment of the Spirit, then the Faithful are called upon to assert their discernment of the Spirit.

The relevancy of the principle of Default Discernment of the Spirit was brought home to pew-Catholics by the scandal of priestly sexual abuse of innocents. The failure of the Hierarchy to heed the Spirit, to pay attention to their conscience, was egregious!

But is there a rule and what is the rule for pew intervention in Hierarchy failures of a lesser impact or of minor matters?

51

## Triggers for Intervention?

How would the pew-Catholic know when and whether he or she ought to intervene in the operation of the Church organization? Clearly, if the Hierarchy sins, then intervention is a must. In fuzzy situations when the Hierarchy appears to take the Church into unclear directions, then subtle discernment is needed. A sound principle for intervention can be found in Aristotle's *Nicomachean Ethics*. The principle is called *epiekeia*. Aquinas adopted the principle, as did other Christian moral theologians. *Epiekeia* recognizes that a law or doctrine is sound. At the same time, it may happen that unforeseen circumstances arise. Following the letter of the law might bring haphazard results. In that specific instance, the law loses its binding power. *Epiekeia* applies when collateral damage from application of the law is expected to cause greater harm than what harm the law was intended to prevent.

For example, let's say it is midnight and I am at my night job. I get a phone call because my house is on fire. I need to be there to oversee proper security and especially to be at the side of my wife and children to comfort and provide for them. On my way home, I find I'm halted at a red stop light. Because it is late, there are no cars in sight anywhere in all directions. *Epiekeia* says I may proceed against the red light. Moreover, to be delayed from providing security and consoling my family as soon as possible is not acceptable when there is no traffic for the red light to regulate. What is obvious: to strengthen my family at times of a fire is more important than to wait at a stop light honoring a law that has no application at the time. *Epiekeia* seems to counsel us in these grey areas. However, applying *epiekeia* to Church operations or doctrine requires sincere thought, lots of prayer, and an open and honest conference within the Faithful before a loving confrontation with the

Hierarchy. The confrontation is to be guided by a search for what is a proper operation or doctrine of the Church and not to win the argument.

## Summary and Conclusion

What is memorable from the discussion of the Council of Constance is as follows: for starters, the Bishops drew out what the full notion of "Catholic" means (i.e., the *sensus fidelium*). Second, with the passage of the *Sacrosancta* the Bishops gave recognition to the need for the *sensus fidelium* of the Bishops in Council as a counter measure to the failures of the Hierarchy. Third, the Hierarchy does not have a monopoly on the Holy Spirit, but the Holy Spirit dwells among the Bishops in Council. Finally, the Faithful need to apply the principle of the Default Discernment of the Holy Spirit when the Hierarchy has obviously ignored the Spirit.

Except in obvious situations of failures by the Hierarchy to heed the Holy Spirit, the principle of *epiekeia* is a legitimate guide to decide whether an intervention in the affairs of the Church is necessary. Proper protocols such as prayer and consultation among the Faithful are necessary to assure a legitimacy to the intervention. Kindness and respect are protocols for every intervention as well as a sound general operating principle.

# CHAPTER FIVE:

## Sources of Reform II

The discussion of sources for reform turns to the Council of Vatican II. The work of the Bishops at that conference is still fresh in the minds of many pew-Catholics. Those Bishops oversaw the development of doctrine. Most doctrinal developments were ignored by the immediately succeeding Popes who had voted with the nay-sayers at the Council, yet the memory of Vatican II now serves to help many pew-Catholics formulate and found their contribution to the synodal process. A significant instance of memory carries the understanding that the outcomes of Vatican II were intended as blueprints, inchoate programs, or prescriptions for action.

**Background to the Council of Vatican II (1962-1965)**

Subsequent to the Council of Constance, the *Sacrosancta* was fought but mostly ignored by popes. Pope Pius IX presided over a Council of Bishops called Vatican I (1869-1870). He used the Council of Vatican I to bury *Sacrosancta* for all practical purposes. Pope Pius IX, concerned about the Church's being abandoned, ignored, or left behind, assigned the Bishops of Vatican I the purpose of defining how the Church was to remain a world player.

The next five paragraphs are repeated from earlier text to emphasize the aggressiveness of Pope Pius IX and its effects on the thinking of the Church. It describes the kind of church that Pope John XXIII ran into the first day of his Papacy—closed to the world with a Hierarchy of stiff-necks comfortable in their presumed infallibility.

An aggressive Pope, Pius also assigned to his consulting theologians the task of developing the schema whereby the Pope may be considered infallible when ruling *ex cathedra* (i.e., speaking officially as and calling attention to his role as the successor of Peter). Pius' idea was to settle aggressively any wavering about the veracity of the Church doctrine. The Bishops of the Council of Vatican I voted the Pope infallible. However, the Council was short-lived. With the start of the Franco-Austrian War in 1859, many Bishops hurried back to their dioceses. Thus, fewer Bishops remained than constitute what would be considered a Council; however, Vatican I, meeting before the start of the war, lasted long enough for the Bishops to enact a decree of infallibility: *Pastor Aeternus* (*The Eternal Pastor*) was voted the authority of the Pope.

Openly, the decree was hailed and praised by members of the Hierarchy, but in secret, some within the Cardinal ranks had severe misgivings. In particular Cardinal John Henry Newman was uneasy, working as he was on his thesis and about to publish *The Development of Christian Doctrine*. Not all in the Hierarchy saw the promulgation of decrees as the way to establish doctrine; they held with Newman that doctrine develops over time with the inspiration of the Spirit expressed in the Faithful. The concerned prelates saw none of that in *Pastor Aeternus*.

Nevertheless, all the clergy and the prelates, the Pope, the Vatican Officers, the Hierarchy, the pastors, and the parish priests began to see themselves as somehow participants in the power of infallibility. They embraced their positions as a team of successors to Peter. They became enamored with the power implied in their position as in place of Peter, and by extension, in place of Jesus and by still another extension in place of God. The priests and bishops found it convenient, even in informal conversation, to imply what they offered was somehow an offshoot of Vatican infallibility. Most clergy easily fell into a way of thinking that as a member of "the team" they were in a position to speak for God; they began to identify themselves, not quickly and explicitly, but slowly and subtly with God. The result was to distance the Hierarchy still further from the pews. Clericalism was strengthened and hit a high point. The thoughts, actions, and attitudes of the Hierarchy revealed a treatment of the Faithful as sheep, to be rounded up by the shepherds. Furthermore, the Hierarchy engaged in *hubris*.

Ancient Greeks portrayed in their tragedies what they considered the ultimate transgression: *hubris*. Their tragedies acted out *hubris*, whereby tragic characters were portrayed possessed of a great talent that caused them to feel an overriding pride. This pride became so deep in their characters they considered themselves to be gods. *Hubris* is a Classical Greek sin of pride out of control; a *hubris* pride is of such arrogance that a person feels no need for accountability; no need to account, not even to the gods!

## The Council of Vatican II

Pope John XXIII called for a "Vatican II" Council of Bishops to be convened in 1962. Papal watchers consider that Pope John had in mind to correct the Vatican I decree or at least to soften the declaration of infallibility.

The late 1870's *ex cathedra* infallibility of Vatican I had become in the 1960's an impediment to the fledgling ecumenical movement. How could a Catholic tell his Lutheran buddy that I respect you as a brother and your religious beliefs, but I am the one who is always right? The priests and Bishops also had problems trying to explain some of the

Magisterium's rulings; for example, the Curia's prohibition of contraception among sincere wedded couples. Contraception was prohibited even after faithful, learned Catholic physicians had spent time going through studies of medical physiologic and psychiatric research—all pointing to conditions allowing for contraception's legitimacy. At the same time, other deeply-researched theological studies resulted in a series of *dubeats* (a legitimate questioning of aspects of doctrine or rulings of the Church). The *dubeats* were generally ignored by the Hierarchy. Pope John XXIII desired to catch up with all the "Becomings" going on around the world. He worried that the Church seemed to be and in fact was standing still in an age when not to "Become" was to fall behind.

## Two Foundational Messages from Vatican II

**Lumen Gentium** (*A Light to the Nations*) opens with the Bishops asserting the principle that the Church is the People of God. This principle countered the clericalism of the Hierarchy. (As a reminder, clericalism is the culture that causes the Hierarchy to consider themselves the Church, superior to other Catholics, and the exclusive recipients of the Holy Spirit.) The decree of the Bishops of the Council certainly addressed clericalism. They decreed that the People of God are filled with the gifts of the Holy Spirit, the *sensus fidelium.* On that basis, Vatican II called the pew-Catholic to the fullness of Church life. Fullness of participation was to include the offices of ministry and administration; the Bishops were clear to link the expression of "a person of whatever rank" to Church office and the "fullness of Christian life."

There were to be no preconceived notions or restrictions about who and what office a child of God may hold. The immediate effect of the

Council was to deal clericalism and its associated privileges a significant blow. The blow was not fatal because the Hierarchy was simply called on to accept the reality of how the Holy Spirit operates. It was only in the Latin of the Bishops, but not in the operation of the Church, the Bishops took away from the Hierarchy its claimed monopoly on the Holy Spirit.

There is still another side to this coin to be spent, however. The pew-Catholics were called to their responsibility to respond to the privilege of enjoying inspirations by the Holy Spirit; to engage fully in the operation of the Church; to give sincerely measured time and treasure and talent to the work of the parish. That, too, was a dream of the Council, perhaps more in the Latin of the Bishops than in the behavior of the pews.

The track record of the pew-Catholic is very uneven. There have been some serious spiritual movements inspired by and carried out by the pew-Catholic. Lay theologians have written of how and why reform is needed in the Church. At the same time, many theologians, if not most, write their challenge to the Hierarchy in peer-judged professional journals or in popular Catholic monthly magazines, but not in actionable letters to their diocesan bishop. Given the unkind reception by the Magisterium of renewed looks at practice and doctrine, theologians have pulled in their *dubeats*. That is totally understandable; heroic virtue is for heroes; some have families to support; you may not demand heroic virtue of another person. And yes, recognition needs to be given to those priests and theologians who have resigned from their ministries because they see unfulfilled needed reform. The point is this: the response of the pew-Catholics and their lay leadership is very uneven. Perhaps, honesty requires the label "poor."

Try a mental experiment. Think about just how much the pew-Catholic is laid back in your parish: Suppose that "X" is a very real problem. Suppose it came up again at Sunday Mass. After Mass, you ask a number of the parishioners to sign up to join you to meet with your Pastor about X. What is your honest estimate of how many volunteers would join you in talking to the Pastor?

Pew-Catholics have been gaslighted; as a result, they are content to be sheep of the shepherd; they will follow the rules and hope to get into heaven. It smacks of an unholy pact between the Hierarchy and the pew-Catholics: "I won't bother you if you don't demand too much of me." Both parties stand accused: the Hierarchy has failed to stimulate the Faithful to participate more meaningfully in witnessing to God; the pew-Catholics have allowed themselves to be "bought" by the Hierarchy for a set of rules to make an easy, minimal-involvement passage into Heaven.

The second lesson is in **Gaudium et Spes** (*Joy and Hope*). A follow-up instruction to *Lumen Gentium,* the instruction explains the People of God are on a pilgrimage to the ultimate formation of the Kingdom at the end of time. Therefore, this instruction draws attention to the work of "becoming" the end-goal of the perfect formation of the People of God. The goal is perfection, and perfection requires change and often. Our work here and now directed to the Kingdom is the "becoming" to which *Lumen Gentium* calls the Faithful. The Faithful are reminded the Kingdom is never finished on earth; the Faithful must always become anew and reform to become closer to the ultimate Kingdom; *ecclesia semper reformanda.*

The Council alerted the pew-Catholic to the dynamics of the world— to change in the world. The People of God are not to be frightened by change; rather they are to see change as a "becoming" in the Church as well as in the world around them. At the second half of the 1900's, people were experiencing rapid and multiple changes—scientists were developing new theorems, nations were sending rockets into space, computers became obsolete at the very time of sale, wireless voice and image were expanding, societal norms were under scrutiny—all affecting the heart and soul of the home and Church. The Bishops urged the people to receive change as an integral process of making the world anew in Jesus. Furthermore, the Bishops urged the people to understand change as an integral part of the process to become the Kingdom.

The instruction urged the pew-Catholics to become deeply studied in their beliefs as to understand how all things fit into God's plan. The instruction relative to the Church went beyond urging. The instruction laid on the pew-Catholic the duty—even the duty to speak out when concerned about the Church. It was clear, *Gaudium et Spes,* acknowledging the Spirit in every believer, asserted knowledge is power: if you notice something, say something. The pew-Catholics are required to speak out because they are partners; therefore, they are responsible for achieving the Kingdom; they may not shrug off the responsibility.

With their culture of clericalism, the Hierarchy decided to fight the instruction of the Bishops of the Council. They carried their negativity into, during, and after the Council; they used operational stubbornness as a strategy to frustrate any change and to anchor in cement their usual practices. Pope John Paul II and Pope Benedict XVI, both recidivist naysayers in the Council's theological debates, deliberately shut down any attempt at change; they censured forward-looking theologians like Hans Küng and Charles Curran. Finally, they insisted Catholics must submit to the Magisterium; they ignored the instruction that allowed all believers to follow freely their consciences. They appointed bishops from clerics whom they screened and knew would be loyal to them. In effect, Popes John Paul and Benedict froze the Church into the status quo.

The status quo negated any promise of "becoming" as understood in the spirit and sense of the Vatican II decree. "Joy and Hope" remained just that: a promise. The major source of reform in the Church, a Council of Bishops, was totally frustrated in its outcomes by two Popes who had lost in the debates among the Bishops.

## Dignitas Humanae

"Dignity of the Human Person" provides the most direct theological base for a respectful recognition of the pew-Catholic. Each person claims status as a Child of God. Secular, civil authority grants everyone dignity on the basis of their personhood. No matter how respectable one may be, the Vatican II decree goes beyond civil recognition; instead, each person's dignity rests in a person's direct relation to God—God's Child. The freedom to follow one's lights stands out. There is no middle man between the person and God, not a Pope, not a Bishop, not a priest. The autonomy of a direct child relation to God constitutes the pew-Catholic as his own jury; the Hierarchy may not coerce, interfere, or even judge. Upon answering to God according to the light of his or her informed conscience, the pew-Catholic may stand comfortably before God and not care about what the Magisterium may think or say. And in the process, the cleric is required to recognize the autonomy of the person's conscience.

Self-rule is wonderful, yet on the other side of the coin is the direct responsibility the child of God must exercise in his or her behavior. No one can accept blame or shame for the Child of God except the Child of God. Sometimes the Hierarchy speaks sarcastically of the freedom of conscience as a "license-to-do-whatever-you-want." In truth, the status of having freedom of conscience carries more responsibility than it does freedom. The so-called "freedom" in the "freedom of conscience" relates to the freedom from any coercion the Child of God is to enjoy in deciding the morality of his or her options. The "conscience" in the "freedom of conscience" relates to the responsibility to choose in accordance with one's conscience, and that implies the responsibility to make sure you have a clear and thorough understanding of the rights and wrongs of what you are about to do. There's not much room for whimsy in that process. What you do must be done with a clear and informed conscience.

Plunked down into the current Church organization, the Child of God faces the Magisterium. The Magisterium insists under current Canon Law that the Magisterium trumps your personal *sensus fidelium*, which is your informed conscience. The bishops and pastors insist Catholics are required to follow the Magisterium's decrees. But that represents a coercion to act in the Hierarchy's way regardless of what one's conscience indicates.

***Dignitas Humanae* requires certain and obvious sections of Canon Law be voided. For example, Canon Law specifies the ruling of the Congregation for Faith trumps the individual conscience of the Child of God. Vatican II erased that Canon. The Bishops of Vatican II fixed the base for personal morality in the status of a Child of God. Reform in the administration of the Church is required. A default position to favor the pew-Catholic in Canon Law needs to be introduced. In the spirit and letter of Vatican II, the Church faces a deep reform in structure, culture, and operation.**

## Take-Aways from the Decrees of Vatican II

We learn from these Vatican II decrees how to situate the pew-Catholic within the Church's current organization. The Church has to be understood as the entire People of God. There need be a radical change in the Hierarchy's culture and conviction that there are two classes of membership; they must see two classes as a contradiction to Jesus' radical equality.

The ordained are to understand Holy Orders as a voluntary self-offering to be the delegate of the people of God witnessing the operations of God's work among us. The ordained become the *servus servorum Dei*, the servant of the servants of God. They now bear the duty of maintaining the past record of the Spirit's whispers; in turn, they must cultivate a mechanism whereby the continuing murmurs of the Holy Spirit are recognized and recorded. They have the delegated responsibility of channeling and assuring the Church continues its becoming the People of God.

Again, the Hierarchy, threatened to the core, will especially fight the idea of being called to serve. It is almost beyond imagination the Hierarchy will surrender the privileges they now enjoy for the duties and responsibilities of service. To watch one's life-ambition and life-achievement washed away involves serious desolation of the self-image, a deep identity change, perhaps identity collapse, a complete ego-dissolution. There probably is no immediate danger of "nervous breakdowns" among high-ranking Vatican officials because the Church does not move that fast. And, depending upon your perspective, this could be fortunate or not, yet the clock is always ticking. Time with gradual turnover in personnel will allow the upcoming prelates a chance to re-elect if they choose; however, the initial reaction of the

Hierarchy will be strong, even bitter resistance turned very ugly and painful. At the same time it is absolutely necessary!

To understand, even to sympathize with, the Hierarchy is possible. Up till now, the pew-Catholics have been enablers. The Faithful, all but a few, allowed the prelates to indulge themselves. But when enablers turn challengers, then resistance to change takes the form of striking out at the former enablers. No one can predict the outcome. Will there be an attempted coup by the Hierarchy? a freeze of all Vatican operation? the equivalent of a strike? a desk-in? a religious service walkout? Reform does demand of the Hierarchy a surrender of their clericalism, their infallibility, their sole possession of the Holy Spirit, their special ordination status, their title as Prince, their purple robes, and their miter hats.

## A Very Important Point

Even if the reforms petitioned by the Faithful are enacted by the Council, the pew-Catholic has not arrived at the land of milk and honey. Flowing immediately from the recognition of the *sensus fidelium* is a call to every pew-Catholic for responsible action. Pope Francis has opened the door to ask of the pew-Catholics: What will you volunteer to begin or carry on or complete in the evangelization program of your parish? Are ushers, readers, or communion assistants needed at Sunday Mass? What might you contribute of your business talent to help the parish unemployed, control the parish expenditures, and teach parish graduates how to interview? What studies or talents do you have to share in the pastor's ministry? to teach Sunday school or the candidates for confirmation? Perhaps you could cover parishioners' hospital admissions? coach the parish youth basketball team? help out in some way in the parish's neighborhood mission? How will you live up to full participation in the Church?

On the other hand, if the Synodal Process yields no reform, if there is no response to the suggestions or demands of the Faithful, who can predict the response of disappointed, long suffering, hope-suddenly-dashed Catholics? especially the Catholic women? Catholic women have suffered patiently, beyond reason, with a male-dominated Church-certified misogyny. They have led a petition for gender-neutral religion, a petition begun in Germany but now migrated to nations around the world. And their men are with them.

**Now What?**

No one can predict whether there will be a sudden mass-exodus from the Church or a creeping attrition signaled by gradual decreases in the amounts given in the weekly contribution envelopes. Will there be more boycotts worldwide? Will some Catholic parishioners attempt to pirate their parish priest; set up what they would consider the real Catholic Church? Is it possible that former parishioners might set up their Spirit enterprise in the parish facilities, ready to fight the diocese in a legal-to-last-many-years battle over ownership of the church and school buildings?

It is expected the response to disappointment by either prelate or pew will be more resentful than welcome, more militaristic than peaceful, more schismatic than unifying. Those who see themselves as losers will make a decision as to what and where to apply pressure. That can be very straining on the nerves and disposition of all participants. Whatever is done will be done and then answered by still another escalation. It's likely any action that will take place will do so without an overarching coordinated plan; here and there perhaps an exception by a unified small scattered group. The reform may end in multiple sects to further fracture hope for the Jesus prayer that they may be one.

## Conclusions from a Review of the Bishops in Council

A Council is called by the Pope. A sitting Pope could decide to reform the Hierarchy and end the second-class status of the pew-Catholic by setting the agenda in calling the Bishops to Rome. Then, the Pope could direct all efforts to the remediation of clericalism, the restructure of the organization, and the revision of the Canons of Law. In fact, a number of deeply concerned Catholics, epitomized by author James Carroll in his *The Truth At The Heart Of The Lie*, looked to Pope Francis for a direct attack on the clericalism of the Hierarchy. Francis was not part of the Vatican crowd; he came with a pastor's soul and a pastor's experience among the hovels of South America; he appeared to be without baggage to weigh him down; and some of his initial behavior as Pope hinted at a possible constraining of the Hierarchy.

**Defenders of Pope Francis might note that if Pope Francis were to act directly, forcefully and unilaterally against the Hierarchy even because of their clericalism, he would be claiming sole possession of the Holy Spirit—precisely what constitutes the error of the clericalism of the Hierarchy. On the other hand, Pope Francis, by calling for the Synodal Process, opens the Church to the *sensus fidelium* into the Catholicity of the Church, the way the Church ought to work. Perhaps most operational, Pope Francis, in calling for another year of issue-curing, shows that he understands to turn the Ocean Liner of Peter around 180 degrees would simply cause the craft to shudder itself apart. Everything in its time.**

The council of Constance provided the first impulse to a universal collegiality by its introspective look at its Catholicity; from their sense of collegiality they formed the Bishops' *sensus fidelium* as the criteria of action for the Papal Offices, the *Sacrosancta.*

Vatican II gave voice to the pews; the Holy Spirit hovers over each of the People of God. Thus, the Council asserted the believers' responsibility to account directly to God without coercion from anyone. Each person holds an immunity, so to speak, from Church Hierarchy, while at the same time is to live and love under an obligation to foster Church witness, the People of God's entire witness to Jesus before the world. The Vatican is to heed the sincere discernment of the Holy Spirit, the *sensus fidelium.* The bedrock of the dignity of the person is the status as a Child of God.

The Councils are the major tools for change in the Church. But with Pope John XXIII's death, a program to install and maintain those decrees and directives of Vatican II was never implemented. Those programs, preserved in the memories of the Faithful and some open-minded Hierarchy, need come from the next assembly of Bishops. We might very well ask: Is the Synodal Process "Vatican III?"

# CHAPTER SIX:

## Sources of Reform III

Thirty years ago, theologians Eugene C. Bianchi and Rosemary Radford Ruether edited a book of essays entitled *Toward a Democratic Catholic Church*. The occasion for which they gathered the essays was the thirtieth anniversary of the Council of Vatican II. The theme of the essays is the question of whether, why, and how should the Church become a democratic institution. Contributors included headliner theologians Hans Küng, Schussler-Fiorenza, Curran, Dolan, Berryman, and the editors themselves. The point then was what this book espouses now: the Church Hierarchy grew into an oligarchy from accidents of history. That is not in keeping with the teaching and life of Jesus, nor with the history of the early church and the Council of Vatican II. All the essays, each from that author's research discipline, pointed favorably toward democratization of the Church. Therefore, editors Bianchi and Radford Ruether were prompted to ask of themselves the question: Who could carry off a movement toward the democratization of the Church?

At the time, two factors were in place for such a moment. First, Vatican II had left a legacy of decrees that formed the theological basis for a democratic Catholic Church. Second, after the Council ended, its legacy was to stir still more in-depth and advanced research by Church theologians and other-disciplined scholars. The theologians and scholars had developed within the Church tradition a body of knowledge and teaching on bishop collegiality, the *sensus fidelium*, the organizational application of subsidiarity, the morality of personal freedom and responsibility, and the dynamics of participation in society. The stage was set for a democratic Act One.

At any rate, the Hierarchy in the persons of the Popes and Curial personnel opposed to Vatican II effectively brought the curtain down on Act One. They made sure that Vatican II thinking, research, or talk would not reach the mass of Catholics—at least a mass of the size required to lobby for and carry out a democratic Act One. Previously noted was the deliberate sabotage by Popes John Paul II and Benedict XVI of any implementation of Vatican II; noted was Notre Dame theologian Father Richard McBrien, his quote openly describing the papacies of John Paul and Benedict as a slow-moving coup of the Church.

Editors Bianchi and Radford Ruether, prompted by the essays of their contributors, raised and then suggested an answer to their question: Who could possibly carry off a movement toward the democratization of the Church? Their thoughtful answer was to hope enough influential and organized pew-Catholics would form an effective coalition of Catholic persona free of any influence from the Hierarchy. Obviously lay folk. The key was to be sure to field influential lay-doers—the committed, able leadership capable of mustering financing and a strong, serious, and action-heavy team to mount a campaign. Such a movement would attract other laity and financing; the movement would become self-sustaining. The job they described was to mold enough of the pew-Catholic opinion to present a universal effort from the pews for action and reform. The goal was to lobby at all levels of the Church, from every parish, through the diocese all the way to Rome; and if necessary, to put muscle into the requests for reform by threats of an organized and ready universal boycott of the Church. The coalition would be the spark and the mover to achieve democratic reforms for the People of God. In a sense, the scandal of the global-wide sexual abuse of innocents by priests and its cover-up has somewhat mobilized the Faithful but along several different issues. That there was no formal mass rebellion means that there still are too many Hierarchy-enablers in the pews.

## A Pew-Catholic Reform Movement

Where does a group start a movement? Where does the lobbying begin and how? Where to gather the Faithful for a meaningful exchange of ideas? Teams generally perform best at their home venues. That logic suggests to start the lobbying at the local parish level, reaching the parishioners through a form of town hall. The members of the audience should not feel any pressure other than to listen and observe; they may join in if they choose. Depending on the stance of the pastor, it seems the parish or school hall ought to be available to parishioners. Given a defensive pastor or one fearful of his Bishop's reaction, the town hall could be held in a local restaurant, bar, or rented public hall or school. The agenda and speakers need to be planned and the topics honed to that set of parishioners. One absolute must: A collection or appeal for funds is not allowed. The movement has to be self-sustaining from the start; the movement needs to develop funding sources, possibly from the founders who themselves enjoy individual wealth, who in turn are able to draw in still more financial backing.

The next step would be a call on the local Bishop. A visit to the Bishop is easier and less expensive than to tackle distant Rome. Further, to choose a reform of a local practice automatically involves the local Catholics and limits the movement to the diocese and the Bishop. The Bishop has a wide range of autonomy even under existing Canon Law. The Bishop may have to be reminded that he does not have to check with Rome on every issue. In his diocese the Bishop is Rome. Of course, the idea is to select that which is within the local Bishop's purview. Why is this plan a good plan? Because it has worked.

## Wheeling-Charleston, West Virginia Diocese

In July of 2019 in the Wheeling-Charleston, West Virginia, Diocese, an example occurred of a successful negotiation by pew-Catholics with a diocese on an important set of local reform issues. William Lori, as an Apostolic Administrator, was appointed to clean up the diocese of Wheeling-Charleston, West Virginia. The deposed Bishop Michael Bransfield had destroyed the diocese financially and, more importantly, he had scandalized the laity to the point they easily called into question the trust and credibility of the entire Catholic Church. Bransfield was financially profligate and a scandal to the church. "That is an understatement," was the sentiment of almost every Catholic in the Wheeling-Charleston diocese. William Lori had a real mess on his hands—a financial and a mismanagement mess he had to clean up.

The West Virginian pew-Catholics had suffered both the profligacy and also the stinging embarrassment of a Bishop who scandalized their Church and their beliefs. They formed a church-membership-local-Catholic organization within the diocese, and called it "Lay Catholic Voices for Change." This group was intent on real change, especially mindful of the financial damage of Bishop Bransfield; they sought genuine reform of the financial oversight in their diocese. They sent a letter to newly appointed William Lori. In the letter, Lay Catholic Voices for Change wrote very specific demands, what concrete measures of reform they demanded. Major reform was specified. The finances of the diocese were to be made public, and a Certified Public Accountant was to be retained for an annual audit.

But here's the point: in the letter Lay Catholic Voices for Change put some real teeth. They threatened to instigate a financial boycott of the diocese if their demands were not met. The threatened boycott was extensive and aimed at six diocesan budgets. They threatened no further contributions to fund the priests' retirement program and not to any other program, even citing the abandonment of the diocesan scholarship fund which would affect their own children. They demonstrated to the diocesan headquarters strong lay leadership, with gravitas and determination, with very specific demands, and with real consequences were they rebuffed.

Of course, the letter got the attention of both Administrator Lori and the Hierarchy who had appointed Mr. Lori. They recognized not only the threat was real but also, given the circumstances of the past, the financial burden of reform would fall on those who had sponsored the letter. Their demands were justified.

The boycott was scheduled to begin on July 21, 2019. The Apostolic Administrator and his Hierarchy recognized they were being seriously and legitimately confronted by sincere West Virginia Lay Catholics. These were the people who were being called upon to foot the bill for the wasteful years of Bishop Bransfields. On July 17, William Lori announced that, among other reforms, a regularized annual CPA audit would be conducted and the finances of the diocese would regularly be made public. Lay Catholic Voices For Change acknowledged Mr. Lori's reply and withdrew the threat and the plans for the boycott.

In this case, the boycott did not have to be carried out; the effectiveness of the threat of a boycott was clear and it was readily recognized the demands were justified. The pew-Catholics used the threat of a boycott to put into place their informed understanding of how a diocese ought to be financially managed. Note that even in what appears as a worldly matter, the finances of the diocese, the pew-Catholics steered the local Diocese toward the realization of the Kingdom; and they did it by respecting themselves and their dignity as Children of God.

It is important to note the demands and threat were firm but respectful. Figuratively, no one threw a Molotov cocktail. However, every dissatisfied Catholic needs to memorize this as though it is a daily prayer: the boycott is to advance the Kingdom. The squabble is an exercise in who has the Spirit and the demands are a cry for the wholeness of the Kingdom. Therefore, to lack charity does not balance a lack of charity; it simply adds to the total loss of love.

**Berlin and the Major Cities of Germany**

Another successful use of the boycott preceded West Virginia. The Catholic Women of Germany conducted a boycott of the entire German Church during the week of May 11-18, 2019. Note: the boycott was of the entire German national episcopacy. The women withdrew their usual volunteer services from the parishes, schools, and other assets in every German diocese for one week. They refused to participate in their usual committee assignments. They did not attend to the bookkeeping, nor the housekeeping, nor the laundering needs of the parish. They did not attend the May 12th Sunday Mass at which they were scheduled to read the liturgical passages. Instead, the women gathered in the courtyards of the Churches; they engaged in prayer, sang hymns, and preached messages of encouragement to one another; it is reported that some even danced in praise of God.

This boycott occurred at fifty locations across Germany, including in the large cities of Berlin and Munster. Across the border, there was an echo of the boycott in Vienna, Austria. Of note is that the women took on the enlarged challenge of reaching the entire German Catholic Hierarchy. The boycott was a success. Not only was the boycott well organized, but it remained orderly, enlisted Catholic males, was specific in its demands, and when it came time for action, was well-executed in each of the locations.

The effective organization of the boycott also showed in the precision of the German women's demands. Their purpose was to turn the attention of the German Hierarchy to five issues: 1) justice for the victims of priestly sexual abuse; 2) a charitable approach to the persons of homosexuals; 3) an optional celibacy in the priesthood; 4) reforms in the German Church's sexual education programs; and 5) inclusion of women in the governance and ministry of the Church.

The women were definitely motivated. They had seen their German Church losing members—at a pace exceeding 100,000 members per year over the prior ten years. In the more recent years, the losses had grown to more than two hundred thousand. Priestly sexual abuse, ultimately known to be a fact and revealed as a scandal, was shaving Church's membership to the bone.

With the German Catholic women exposed to and regularly aware of the women ministers in other denominations, Catholics recognized the importance of addressing the growing impatience among their young ladies with aspirations to a priestly vocation. More and more young women felt the call to the altar, heard the Holy Spirit, and were prepared to embrace their call as a child of God.

Another observation, that of the Church sometimes publicly denigrating persons on the basis of their different sexual orientation, was brought forward. Further, the growing shortage of priests called the women's attention to well-balanced healthy young men of talent, some their sons, who were potential priests but were deterred by the celibacy requirement. And not the least of dissatisfactions was the misogyny baked into the Church practices. The women had schooled themselves, done the research, determined the pretzel-contorted mind games proposed by the Hierarchy to prohibit women from office and ministry were without any merit. They understood intellectually, scripturally, and historically the Hierarchy offered empty arguments, proving nothing but the misogyny of the male ministers. The women sought to introduce the *sensus fidelium* of the German Catholics into the formal Church.

What is very clear is the German women's boycott was respectful of the Hierarchy, but it is also very clear that it carried the firmness of the *Willensstarke Frau*. The lesson to be learned here: the demands are to be respectful but never "wishy-washy." Although the German women were firm, they nevertheless showed an understanding of the position of the Hierarchy; they took account of their Bishops' Vatican oversight. They simply started the discussion that would get Church-wide attention. They estimated correctly an understanding of the issues might evolve into a conviction in the mind of the Prelates. They knew these matters would necessarily involve Rome, and so they drew no guns; they hurled no daggers into the negotiating table; but they drew serious attention to what needed to be changed.

The boycott was successful: the women were heard and a synodal-like conference between the Bishops and the laity ensued with an agenda devoted to their issues as well as to concerns of the Bishops. The Hierarchy was represented at the gatherings by no less than a Cardinal, His Eminence Reinhard Marx. Actually, any successes associated with the synodal-like meetings are his. A pioneering prelate, he managed to organize, working with four different German Catholic Associations, a synodal-like conference. The recommendations of these synodal-like talks are positive. There remains at least one more session to be held. The final vote on the chosen issues will be the ultimate scoreboard.

What has been welcomed by most of the German Hierarchy is not welcomed universally among Church leadership. Of course the Curia and the Pope have been keeping an eye on Germany and the developments of those meetings. The Vatican fear is the Hierarchy may be <u>too</u> understanding of the pew-Catholics and result in a breakaway German Church.

In addition, seventy Bishops from four Continents are also watching and have gone so far as to express their concern in an open letter to the German Hierarchy. Their fear is what the German Hierarchy is doing will necessarily lead to a schism. Those seventy, in their fear for reform, have already made a judgment that the German Bishops will vote for the reform issues raised by the Catholic women.

**Triggers to Action**

Pew-Catholics are confronted with mixed emotions when the conversation turns to problems with prelates or pastors. When and why are the folks in the pews to take action and intervene in Church matters and especially on the running of the Church? One suggestion is this: the principle of "Default Discernment of the Spirit." Think about it. If the Hierarchy defaults in its governance (i.e., has not or will not follow the obvious guidance of the Spirit), then the Faithful are to implement their guidance, the *sensus fidelium.* Obviously, if the Hierarchy does something sinful, an intervention is required.

Going forward, the pew-Catholic is left with the questions: How obvious does the failure of the Hierarchy need to be? What triggers a legitimate intervention by a coalition of the Faithful? Must all triggers be a specific action by the Hierarchy? Some examples of triggers to action are offered:

1.  If the officials of the Church exhibit a pattern of not accepting the *sensus fidelium*; for example, they regularly deny the right of pew-Catholics to challenge the Magisterium;

2.  If the Hierarchy insists on a rule, or moral position that will inflict greater harm than the law was meant to serve; or they are in a position to rectify an evil outcome but do not act;

3.  If they interfere in a person's direct relationship with God; or they violate a law of any kind; or they secretly accept or remit funds with the purpose of avoiding proper disclosure.

**Conclusion**

Intervention by the Faithful is required when conditions, events, or rulings of the Church occur to reveal a serious fracture or lack of correspondence between the *sensus fidelium* of the People of God and that of the Hierarchy. The recent very sad scandal has taught the pew-Catholic never to discount its sense of what is right and what is wrong. You have eyes to see and you have ears to hear. Finally, the principle of *epiekeia* is a sound approach to intervention when buttressed by prayer and sincere consultation among the Faithful. This approach automatically includes a group of Catholics as opposed to a single person's approaching the Pastor or Bishop.

# CHAPTER SEVEN:

# The Battlefields

The Office coordinating the Synodal Process, headed by Cardinal Mario Grech, has issued a tally of the views expressed by pew-Catholics scattered in meetings all over the world. Each national Conference of Bishops is presumed to have received the tally. A sense of Catholicity surrounds the tally; it represents what the People of God from around the globe consider the status of the Church. In a true sense it is an organized presentation of the worldwide *sensus fidelium*. An argument can be made the tally represents what the Holy Spirit wants for the Church as expressed through the sentiments of the People of God. Further, it is not a one-sided report; the cautious and negative sentiments surrounding issues are added and presented in the reported tally.

## The Known Backdrop of Battle

Before the Church debates any issue, we know an atmosphere of contention hovers over the Synodal Process. In some, perhaps many, national bishop conferences the reception of Cardinal Grech's tally-report will be met by baked-in attitudes and mindsets. In fact, even the tally-report includes some expressed mindsets regarding the issues. With each issue cited, the report indicates how it was viewed by the reporting diocese. A read of the report indicates those expressed views signal a battle is coming. The dioceses differ among themselves on various issues; there is no one mind. Also, the report highlights the differences between the Hierarchy and the Faithful. For example, the section dealing with the issue of women's Holy Orders titled "Enlarge the Space of Your Tent," tells of starkly diverse stances on whether the priesthood is to be extended to the female membership. Surprisingly, some of the national bishop conferences actually call for its implementation, but other national bishop reports are emphatic in labeling women's ordination as a closed, not-to-be-discussed issue. There will be serious fighting at the Assembly of Bishops unless such diverse views reconcile before the final assembly—which has now been postponed to 2024 by Pope Francis. But the working papers for the First Session of the Assembly of Bishops has been elaborated from the tally. The working papers official title is listed below:

XVI Ordinary General Assembly of the Synod of Bishops
INSTRUMENTUM LABORIS
For First Session
(October, 2023)

The document begins with a forward:

"May the God of endurance and encouragement grant you to think in harmony with one another, in keeping with Christ Jesus, that with one accord you may with one voice glorify the God and Father of our Lord Jesus Christ" (Rom 15:5-6)

Note is made of its origin of composition:

"This Instrumentum Laboris (IL) was drafted on the basis of all the material gathered during the listening phase, and in particular the final documents of the Continental Assemblies."

And then the working paper presents the topics to be taken up by the Bishops, each in a question form. For example, a topic prominent in almost every Synodal Process is thus couched:

Worksheets for B 2. Co-responsibility in Mission

"B 2.3 How can the Church of our time better fulfill its mission through greater recognition and promotion of the baptismal dignity of women?"

The working paper is lengthy and the bishops are not going to lack for topics to discuss and decide. That leads to the possibility of contention in the discussions. The entrenched culture of the Hierarchy—the history of their privileges and their absolute conviction that their ordination grants them a special discernment of the Holy Spirit—all that says the Hierarchy in its majority is opposed to reform. However, some of the Hierarchy are not totally in sync with the others and are vocal about their positions. A battle will ensue behind closed Vatican doors. That battle may possibly carry over into the formal Assembly of Bishops. The battlefields in the Vatican appear to be taking shape.

Added to the background of the Synodal Process are the restless lay petitioners. They have advanced their initiatives on the Council. For example, the determined Catholic women of Germany, with their effectiveness for planning, organizing and implementing, have taken advantage of the Pope's invitation to voice their petition formally within the structure of the Church. They will be joined by Catholic women from around the world. Consider the difference between the Catholic woman from the 1800's during the time of Vatican I and infallibility and today's Catholic woman, who is sophisticated in all walks of life: She has experienced success in major roles of government, science, and commerce; she is sophisticated in Church law, and is more than competent in the practice and theory of organizations, theology of doctrine, and even the judicial basis of Canon law. The Catholic women will persist until the Hierarchy understands and accepts their petition-demands.

## A Papal Postponement

Pope Francis decided to postpone the formal conclusion of the Synodal Process from 2023 to 2024. Francis has to be aware of the entrenched positions and likely is praying and hoping the intervening year will produce some form of resolution if not reconciliation. Leading up to and during that extra year, those serious-minded and motivated opposing factions will be contending literally for the heart, soul, and control of the Church. With the Church at stake, an intense and (hopefully) holy battlefield will occupy the Vatican. Expressions by opponents on both sides of some issues are not gracious and may be seen as demeaning. All are good reasons for Pope Francis to postpone the Assembly of Bishops. A skeptic might attribute the postponement to the need for the Curia to develop some kind of an "out" for the Pope, now that the strength and intensity of the lay's participation has been revealed. But no such "out" has been forthcoming.

## The Pew-Catholic Awakens?

Many pew-Catholics are watching this novel Church event with curiosity. Many note a lot of what is reported reflects how they think. The pew-Catholics perhaps are awakening to their inclusion and their expectations as followers of Jesus. Perhaps more might join in the lobbying of the Hierarchy, but that full spiritual awakening is yet to be seen and effected. What might happen is one of the battlefields of the Vatican assembly becomes an interest of special meaning to awaken the Catholics, perhaps some serious disagreement among the participants with a twist that offends their sense of justice or logic, a nonsense as a theological position. But no issue will bring Catholics into the streets of the Vatican.

## Where is Pope Francis?

Pope Francis still gives mixed signals. Right now, the pew-Catholic still hears from the pulpit a very legalistic religion with emphasis on a set of rules about what you need to do to get to heaven. That is unlike how Pope Frances tends to operate. Pope Francis is trying to swing the pendulum to a more pastoral approach. Instead of asking, "Did you go to Church on Sundays?" Francis might ask, "This morning, did you ask Jesus to bless your day?"

The two different approaches will play a part in the outcome of the Synodal Process. The Hierarchy's clericalism is the source of the legalistic, juridical approach to ministry. The pews have to be kept busy with and dependent on the rules and laws. Presumably, Pope Francis will espouse the opposite, pastoral approach.

In calling for the Synodal Process, Pope Francis seems to harken back to Vatican II, e.g., *Gaudium et Spes* issues a command to the pew-Catholic to speak out about the becoming of the Kingdom. Vatican II also includes a command that the Hierarchy listen to what the lay persons have to say. In calling the synod, Pope Francis has provided an open microphone to the pews, and he has urged repeatedly the Hierarchy truly listen to the pews—with their hearts.

But Francis has been giving mixed signals. In an interview with the Jesuit magazine, *America*, Pope Francis simply repeated the traditional arguments to assert the ordination of women is a closed issue. Francis utters "closed" at the very time he is urging the national bishop conferences to be "open" when considering the given tally of issues that includes women's ordination.

As reported in National Catholic Reporter, Professor Marinella Perroni called out Pope Francis: it seems the Pope walks right past the negative, possibly sinful, consequences of the Hierarchy's position—specifically the Church practices misogyny as the collateral damage of a buttoned-down reasoning that women do not or cannot image Jesus. Retired from her post as Professor of Biblical Theology at the Pontifical Athenum of St. Anselm in Rome, Perroni suggests Pope Francis is "struggling to free himself from the Patriarchal Vision." Professor Perroni notes in espousing the traditional position denying women-ordained ministry, Pope Francis espouses and tries to justify his position with a metaphor that stereotypes the female; therefore, it fosters misogyny. Recall *epiekeia*? Professor Perroni is using it against the Pope's argument: the rule of male-only priesthood, assuming it is valid, has the effect of causing misogyny. Pope Francis is looking for wiggle room but Professor Perroni took it away. Right now, there is no going back for the Pope. Forward is the only direction but Pope Francis is acting like the surgeon in the middle of a surgery who just now said, "oops."

## The Vatican Battlefields

*Who Owns the Holy Spirit*

Thus far the preliminary discussion offers a general outline of what battlefields to expect in the Vatican. Most Hierarchy will defend their sole and exclusive access to the Holy Spirit. That represents their power and privileges that they must protect from a pew takeover. The pew-Catholic will seek reforms to have their *sensus fidelium* recognized. The ownership of the Holy Spirit will form the basic contention and be most intense. What if both owned the Holy Spirit?

## Centralized Power

After the sexual-abuse scandal, the pew-Catholics will want a say in the operation and direction of the Church. The Hierarchy will most certainly resist; in some instances their very livelihood is under attack; for others, the simple adrenaline surge or prestige in exercising power is most important. The attitude that gives support to a centralized power is the culture of clericalism, in which the hallmark tenet is that the unordained are not capable of discerning what is needed in the operation and worship of the Church. The fear of the "old timers" is that Pope Francis will decentralize the Church, but Francis has not committed fully one way or another concerning centralized power.

## Clericalism

The culture that supports the centralization of power will be a battleground because it needs to be willingly surrendered by the Hierarchy or denied to them by moral suasion or rule. Willingly is not a likely scenario, but denial by way of some moral suasion or force may be the only way. In any event, the latter suggests a very bitter battle from the Hierarchy. If the Hierarchy maintains its culture of clericalism, it may appear to agree to what the pews put forward but it will be meaningless.

## *Women Catholic Priests—This Will Be a Big One*

Holy Orders for women has been a battlefield and will peak during the Synodal Process. The seven continental responses to the Document for the Continental Stage were clear that women are ill-treated, even ignored, by the Church. The Working Instrument may be ready for greater recognition of women, while not ready to offer women the full recognition of their baptismal charism: maybe—a big maybe—diaconate now but only a squiggle room—a really big squiggle room—when it comes to priesthood.

There is good reason to wager that a bold ploy instigated by the women will draw special attention to the question of women priests when it surfaces in the Assembly of Bishops. The contention might hit new heights during the Assembly of Bishops. We know the working papers introduce the question of the status and role of women in the Church, and hence women priests will be one of the battlefields in that the Catholic women have already shown their demands with an ability to press the Hierarchy on that issue.

Pope John Paul II tried to stay the inevitable by issuing a Papal letter prohibiting Church officials from even discussing the topic of Holy Orders for women. Such obvious and calculated exclusion of a class within the Church is hard to explain given women make up better than half of the membership. Actually, the present-day exclusion of women from Holy Orders is a continuation of a Church history of misogyny.

Meanwhile, the women of the Church quietly and tirelessly have gone about teaching in the Catholic schools and colleges; serving the health of the Community as aides, nurses, and physicians; cleaning the altar cloths, dusting the pews, and organizing the operation of the Parish office. Nevertheless, committed as they are to the operation and well-being of the Church, the Catholic women truly feel the discriminatory sting of the Hierarchy's misogyny. The posture of many Catholic women at this point of history appears to be now or never; either welcome us in or we'll stay out.

Consider the determination in these excerpts from the letter of the German women announcing the boycott in May of 2019:

"From Saturday, the 11th until Saturday the 18th of May we will not enter the church but deny our service to the church. We want to make known how empty the churches will be without us and how much important work will be unfinished without us.

- We will remain outside. We will dance, sing, pray and find new word and expressions.
- We will celebrate worship together on the church squares, in front of the church gates.
- We will welcome all to participate, also men.
- We will bring white sheets and cover the church squares in the color of innocence, the color of grief and compassion. We will use these sheets to paint, write, combine, stain and create with all ideas welcome as a collection."

*Day Of Action, June 29, 2002—Women Ordained Priests*

How determined are the women? *The action of women measures* the readiness, strength, impatience, and determination of Catholic women. On June 29, 2002 *seven women were ordained priests by Archbishop Romundo Brashi,* and they offered their motivation in a press release:

*"It is a protest against doctrine and church law which discriminates against women."*

The ordination by Bishop Brashi was followed by a confirming ordination by Bishop Felix David, who was ordained Bishop with Vatican approval during WWII by his local bishop in Czechoslovakia. The women, careful to assure their standing, took all necessary steps to declare their ordination as valid and licit.

Ordinations of women are occurring regularly around the world. No fanfare is required, simply the solemnity and reverence due the Holy Spirit. Mary E. Hunt, co-director of Women's Alliance for Theology, Ethics, and Ritual [WATER], explicitly stated the foundation for woman priests in a National Catholic Reporter commentary. Hunt apparently quoted her Marquette University Theology Professor, Fr. Tad Gussi, S.J., who is reported to have said, "A Eucharist celebrated without a priest is a Eucharist celebrated without a priest."

The decree of the Counsel of Trent is encapsulated in that sentence: the effectiveness of a sacrament derives from *ex opere operandum* (the performance of the act). God's invisible blessings descend on us by the simple intent and outward action associated with the outward sign of the Sacrament. For example, a baby becomes a Child of God simply by pouring the water and reciting the formula. Often, we hear of Grandmas who, in fear for their grandchild's imminent death, perform baptisms to assure heaven for the baby.

Trent went further and sternly. Trent decreed that anyone who says you need a priest, *ex opere operantis* (the performer of the act) is a *heretic and excommunicated.* Therefore, "A Eucharist without a priest is a Eucharist without a priest."

Trent provided an answer to a very specific question and concern of people at the time: Did I really and truly receive the grace of the Sacrament if the priest who is performing the sacrament is in mortal sin? Trent's response: It doesn't matter. The outward sign, those symbolic acts and intent prescribed for the Sacrament are what brings God's unseen action upon us. The power lies in the outward sign and intent. The priest simply is a symbol of the God-community's witness.

## Divorced and Remarried Catholics

Couples with a divorced and remarried Catholic partner are received differently by different dioceses. Some bishops insist on the annulment procedures. Other bishops do not even care or worry about the issue. The result is whether restrictions on the reception of Communion are in place or not. Most Catholics and some Bishops delegate the matter to the consciences of the affected individual Catholics. The issue is that certain Cardinals, Bishops and Curial Officials insist on treating those folks as a serious problem. Their stated worry is for a grave scandal in the parish. But is it employment? Some Curia offices would have to close up. Critics of the Curia know the formal annulment is not necessary. It's a Church law, but remember not eating meat on Friday? Is it the Cardinals' and Bishops' simple desire to keep a job? This issue may not arouse much of a battle but it is indeed an issue.

## Charity Toward LGBTQ+

It is anyone's guess just how intense a battle will take place over the stance of the Church toward homosexuality and other gender variations. Presently, one movement is afoot regarding the treatment of the person of gender fluidity; it stems from an argument regarding what pastoral approach is suited and best. But there's another movement, theological in nature, that questions the adequacy of the presuppositions of the Church's theological teaching on sexual morality: Does the Church's underlying understanding of humans in its sexual moral teaching match the reality of humans?

The treatment of homosexuals at the Church door will be silenced by a pastoral approach and be readily resolved. Everyone will agree that Charity must be the formal pastoral approach to persons of gender variability as it is to all persons.

The real and deep question is the adequacy of the Church's presuppositions to the theology founding the Church's teaching and practices on sexual morality. Theologians have published several *dubeats* regarding the presuppositions. The point of the *dubeats* is that the current presuppositions buttressing the church's teaching on sexual morality do not apply to real human people. They stress the "human" in "human sexual practices." Simply put, the *dubeats* argue the Church treats human sexual expression as though people were animals, simply an engagement of cow with the county bull. They argue the Church morality has to apply to a human being, an integral human person.

The Magisterium, up to now, simply has refused to engage those theologians espousing the *dubeats*. These theological differences are ripe for a very intense and sophisticated theological battle involving the nature of man as understood in modern medicine and psychiatry. The battle could start at this juncture in the Vatican.

**Conclusion**

Pope Francis unintentionally (?) but officially started a Vatican Battle by calling for the Synodal Process. The issues raised in the formal

Synodal Process have become the battlegrounds anticipated in a theological tug-of-war between the Vatican offices and pew-Catholics. The pews claim insight into what is needed to advance the Kingdom. Responding to the call of Vatican II for their full participation in the life of the Church, the pews are now asserting their discernment for a share of leadership in the Church. But the influential Cardinals, Bishops and the Curia claim an exclusive access to the discernment of the Holy Spirit; further, they seem to claim that there is no Holy Spirit among the pews. That is the basic battle in the coming Synodal Process, a battle serious for both the pew and the pulpit, but most serious for the Church.

Pope Francis faces a formidable task. He has postponed the formal voting assembly of the Synodal Process to 2024. That's quite reasonable considering the risks involved in this process. Without exaggeration the very unity of the Roman Catholic Church is at risk in this Synodal Process. Both the Hierarchy and the pew-Catholics consider their insights a moral imperative and their denial will have sure but unknown consequences.

The Pope has to consider the unthinkable. What might result in or prevent a major schism of the Church? Could there be even a small schism—a case of a breakaway group who are satisfied to be with like-minded religious folks? or a major fall-off? What if the petition for women's ordination fails, how does the Vatican operate without a breakaway group that now seems to represent the hardworking, serious, contributing half of its membership? If there is no place for the deeply-involved, actively-engaged pew-Catholic in Church governance, does the Hierarchy end up with pews full of folks who are what they consider them to be—mice programmed by Church rules to run a defined morality and liturgical maze?

Pope Francis will need a big dose of the Holy Spirit to work through all the battlefields. Francis faces a divided Hierarchy, a Curia on site and very powerful among the Cardinals and Bishops. Pope Francis also faces a theologically sophisticated laity. They offer serious, legitimate critiques of the style and substance of the Church that when corrected would create sweeping changes in the way the Church operates.

# CHAPTER EIGHT:

## Why Did Pope Francis Call a Synod?

After the doors closed behind the last Cardinals and Bishops of the Vatican II Council, some changes were visible in the Catholic Church—using the local language in the Mass and priests facing the pews. But the Bishops of Vatican II had left a lot of "to-dos" on the table. Only the basic principles and ideas had been put in place: the Church belongs to everyone, who must become seriously involved in it. The Holy Spirit guides the People of God by inspirations and those inspirations carry a responsibility to act. The Hierarchy are to listen to the Faithful with respect, understanding that as Children of God the pew-Catholic enjoys access to the Spirit expressed as the *sensus fidelium*.

There were many leftover to-dos. Those and many currently debated rest on the work of the Bishops in Vatican II—issues already mentioned like optional celibate status for priests, the status of women in the Church, and married-divorced-remarried Catholics. There is also one special note: Pope John XXIII's successor, Pope Paul VI, under very strong pressure from the Curia, nixed the use of contraceptives by serious and responsible Catholic couples. The Curia denied their use even though a committee of the Bishops of Vatican II, in counsel with a professional corps of medical advisors, had declared it moral under specific conditions.

Vatican II was also a resounding success as an ecumenical event. It stirred up great hope and enthusiasm among the non-Catholics as well as lay Catholics. But in the end, Pope John's hopes for the Council were unrealized; none of the decrees were put into operation; in fact, they were squashed. The real work of the Council simply lay there on the table in the Vatican's garage.

Pope Francis' interest in following up on Vatican II can be seen in his recent appointment of Bishop Victor Manuel Fernandez to head the Office of Protector of the Faith. Bishop Fernandez, in his prolific authorship, has embraced the same theological themes and urgency as offered by the Bishops of Vatican II in seeking to engage the world.

In Pope Francis' letter to Bishop Fernandez upon his appointment to head the Congregation for the Faith, Francis calls on Fernandez to stress the "meaning of existence, especially in the face of the questions posed by the progress of the sciences and the development of society." This echoes Vatican II's urging of the Faithful to see the developments in society and sciences as part of God's plan. Pope Francis then offers a serious reason—to "permit us to enter in conversation with 'our present situation,' which is in many ways unprecedented in the history of humanity."

Reaction of those opposed to Pope Francis, his appointment of Fernandez, and his pastoral approach points to the coming Vatican battle of bishops: The web site "*novusordowatch*" appears to categorize Francis' Papacy as a theological freak show. And *Crisis* magazine seems to categorize Francis' Papacy as a program that is about to undermine Catholicism.

Two Popes, John Paul II and Benedict XVI, both of whom had voted against the major schema of Vatican II, made sure the work of the Council was not brought forward to be built upon. One strategy was to intimidate theologians. Two who were not intimidated were Hans Küng and Charles Curran. The Vatican censored them and almost took away their livelihoods by removing their *licentiates* (licenses) to teach as Catholic theologians. The Vatican managed to hide its lack of follow-up to Vatican II behind a curtain of the Pope John Paul II Roadshow. Thus, stadiums filled with Catholic youth greeted Pope John Paul II in cities around the world. His successor, Pope Benedict XVI, no less opposed to Vatican II, was definitely the research and scholarly type, and hardly suited for a Roadshow Papacy. Pope Benedict literally retired from the Papacy, yet prior to doing so Benedict and his papal predecessor had stacked the roll of bishops with men who also opposed Vatican II and preferred a strict, by-the-book legalistic Catholic Church.

A Jesuit priest and Bishop from South America, Pope Francis took charge of the Church. The new Pope acts like the plain folk he served, such as driving his car across town to pay his hotel bill the morning after he was elected Pope. That immediately endeared him to most pew-Catholics. He made it clear immediately from the start his Papacy would be different from the recent past two. He was a pastor who knew the hovels of Sao Paulo and had not forgotten from where he came. He became a symbol of the difference between what is pastoral and what is legalistic. His folksy habits made him dear to some, but also made him suspect to others. Prelates in the Curia and from around the world did not appreciate his pastoral approach; they were more interested in maintaining an aura of ultramontanism (i.e., the infallibility of the Magisterium with powerful influences across the globe). Their hope of maintaining and enhancing ultramontanism was squashed by a Pope who chose an apartment of modest square feet instead of the Lateran Palace.

## The Main Event: Who Has Access to the Holy Spirit?

To generalize, what is at stake here is the claim of the Hierarchy that they have exclusive access to the inspirations of the Holy Spirit. Unless you are ordained and have the unction of a Church office, you have no formal claim to the Holy Spirit. Therefore, you cannot be orthodox. You must be under some self-deception to think that you are following an inspiration of the Holy Spirit. You must be claiming an inspiration of your own misguided making.

That claim becomes a problem because the Bishops of Vatican II decreed the Spirit resides in and guides every Child of God. Therefore, the formal Catholic Church is faced with reconciling, somehow, those two apparently contradictory positions. The overwhelming question is this: Does the Hierarchy possess an exclusive and sacred access to the Holy Spirit or does every Child of God possess access to the Holy Spirit? If there is no mutual resolution, then confrontation is inevitable. Confrontation is scary. No one wants a split in the Church, and surely not one spelled S-C-H-I-S-M!

The decision of Pope Francis to call for a postponement of the general assembly of the Bishops makes a lot of sense. He must be conscious of the expressions of possible challenges to existing Church practices. Pope Francis, like any person conscious of the work of Vatican II, sees the proposals for reform by the pew-Catholics to be the whispers of the Holy Spirit, the *sensus fidelium*. Conscious of Vatican II, those pew-Catholics offering the proposals are very much aware their suggestions are whispers of the Holy Spirit.

Pope Francis has already experienced significant opposition to his call for the Synod. The very process to ask the pew-Catholic for his or her insight is a contradiction of the position of the Hierarchy. Segments of the Cardinals and Bishops, practically all of the Curia, have already gone on record and not only are firmly opposed to the Synodal Process but also have singled out many of the specific suggestions of the Faithful. Pope Francis did not want to air out in the open before the whole world any contentious behavior over the discernment of who holds the Holy Spirit. The postponement makes perfect sense.

## Jesuit Murray and Pluralism at Vatican II

What Pope John XXIII wanted from his Council was an answer to a multifaceted question: How does the Church keep up with the almost universal, fast-paced developments of a self-centered world impressed by and caught up in its progress? How to understand the world with its liberalism and its modern civilization, yet a world troubled by leftover factions from two world wars? John XXIII wanted a platform from which the Church could take off into a world of the 1960s-and-beyond.

Jesuit Father John Courtney Murray accepted Pope John's invitation for a role as the Pope's *peritus* (a Prelate's staff member steeped in a specific discipline). Fr. Murray's specialty was precisely the Church-State relationship as evidenced in his book *We Hold These Truths To Be Self-Evident*. Further, Fr. Murray understood, as did the Pope, there was no way for one Council to establish the platform and also to elaborate in detail the various paths off the platform into the future. Murray's understanding has been confirmed by testimony from his scholarly and ministerial contemporaries; they report that he viewed the work of Vatican II as programmatic. To that end, Pope John tried to get the Bishops to have the most complete view of what he wanted, which was to place the Church of the mid-1960s within a workable framework for its relevance in the modern world.

Fr. Murray saw the possibilities and the perils of the Church as a "Second State" within a State. Recall that until the Christians came on the scene, each State was monolithic; there was the State and there was the State. Christians came on the scene and there was the State and there was the Kingdom of God. Within the State emerged a group claiming allegiance to a Kingdom, a State-not-the-State. The Caesars recognized that immediately and fed the Christians to the lions.

Fr. Murray had observed and understood, and wrote about how even a flourishing role for the Church was possible and in fact realized in a pluralistic State, the United States of America. With that background, his observations, analysis, and understanding proved useful to the Council. He offered the key for the Church to maintain, and in some areas to regain, relevancy in the world: freedom of conscience. Fr. Murray had seen in the U.S. the freedom of citizens based on the recognition of each individual as a person. He offered an operating principle of freedom from coercion based on the dignity and worth of the child of God as a Child of God. But he also offered what is as important, its corollary: the responsibility to be a Child of God, to be the one to answer to God the Father for one's freedom. The dignity of a child of God and the individual's self-responsibility were the platforms on which to install the Church going forward and the key to the *aggiornamento*, the new beginning that Pope John XXIII had in mind.

Many in the Curia saw it another way: Fr. Murray offered what appeared to be the very heart of liberalism as the way forward for the Catholic Church, but there was a world of difference. Fr. Murray offered the sanctity of the individual conscience in the person of a Child of God with the responsibility of accountability to God the Father. No one is permitted to interfere between God and God's child, the basis for the freedom of the conscience, because the Child is accountable, has the responsibility to answer to the Father. The Childhood is the basis for the freedom but more importantly for the responsibility of the conscience. That's totally unlike the political society where rights of the person are asserted ad nauseam and no one knows how to spell "responsibility."

Sometimes we hear a Bishop belittle the concept of freedom of conscience with descriptions such as, "They think that they can engage in all sorts of whimsy and do whatever pleases them." This stereotypical description from those opposed to freedom of conscience in the Church is totally false. The child of God carries heavy responsibility in standing alone before the Father.

**Pope Francis Attracted to Vatican II**

Vatican II was then; Synodal Process is now. There is no identification of one with the other Council. The now is not the then. The now is not simply a readiness of spirit but a preparedness of scholarship and theology. What has changed are not the decrees of Vatican II but the wait and work for their implementation. Now represents an accumulation of sixty-years of anticipated preparedness. Vatican II then promised a new stirring of the Spirit throughout the Church, especially among the pew-Catholics; at last, the Holy Spirit has been cut loose among us. Those of the People of God who followed and took seriously the workings of Vatican II were ready then. They have been patient and stayed with a Spirit-less Church for sixty years. The pew-Catholics have had more time than needed to think and imagine a Spirit-filled Church. Pope Francis enters the Papacy and by his presence and off-the-cuff remarks now creates a remembrance of *aggiornamento*.

The thoughts and hopes left over from Vatican II, are being allowed out and into the open under new management. Theologians such as Küng, Murray, and Curran did much homework during and immediately after Vatican II, thereby creating theological offshoots from the schema of that Council. Thirty years after Vatican II, theologians were ready to revisit the implications of the work of the Bishops of that Council in the publication *Toward A Democratic Catholic Church*. That readiness of thirty years ago has been conserved and multiplied exponentially now.

There is no secret Pope Francis seems attracted to the workings of Vatican II. In fact, that attraction to Vatican II labels him suspect in some conservative Church circles. Pope Francis appears strong, perhaps adamant, in his outright ban of the old Latin Mass. His remarks often reference the work of Vatican II. Some Catholic circles go so far as to wonder if Pope Francis might be the Pope of Vatican III. What is clear is Francis' call for the pew-Catholics to speak their mind to the Hierarchy.

The pew-Catholics have answered the call—in spades! That may very well be a problem. Church-speed is slow and slower. There is no blame for the hurry the pews show in wanting to get their oars into the water. They've been waiting sixty years, but the Faithful may have created a problem for Pope Francis that will turn into a problem of their own. The Faithful have sprung more "becomings" on the agenda of the Synodal Process than might be handled in five decades at Church-speed. Perhaps the first act of the Bishops in Council might be to set time limits on deliberations by the Curia. Perhaps the Church itself must adapt to the speed of today's computers.

Each and every one of the agenda items that have been tallied and reported to the national conferences of Bishops would normally take several years just to be noticed. Then, the debate and prayer in the ordinary schedule and timeline of the Vatican Curia would take several more years. What to do? Under the timeline of the Synodal Process, when called to order, the General Assembly of Bishops in Council are to be charged with deciding what would normally take many years. How do you dispatch these serious reforms in a session—or even five sessions? Just consider the following well-known agenda items: the Ordination of Women, Optional Celibacy for Priests, Blessings on Neo-Gender Morality, and Revisions of Sexual Moral Teachings. This is not softball.

Of course, the point might be made the Councils do not have an end date as such. They may go on and have gone on for years. The Councils are subject to no timelines, except a very important constraint—the lifespan of the Pope who called the Council. There's the rub. Rumors of Pope Francis' retirement or his physical incapacity have been circuiting. Perhaps those Prelates supporting Francis' Council need to learn how to spell "life support." But Francis has asserted his determination to the Papacy as a lifetime appointment. Pope Francis has postponed the General Assembly of Bishops by one year, not a surprise. Given the multitude and flavors of the loaves that await the heat of the oven, not to have postponed the General Assembly would have been mismanagement.

Other speculation on the postponement has it that certain influential Cardinals want nothing to do with Francis' synodal process. What they have heard and seen already is in no way ever going to be approved. So why even discuss it? Some of the Hierarchy decided simply to dig in their heels, and are on record as saying they want to "dismiss" the synodal process. They want to continue the past into the future.

Thus, to summarize: Pew-Catholics are impatient after having been patient for sixty years waiting for the implementation of their hopes from Vatican II. Now they have overwhelmed the Synodal Process with studied requests for reforms that would normally be in process for more years than can reasonably be expected of a single Council in the slow-moving Vatican grinder. That gives Pope Francis cause to pause the meeting of the General Assembly of Bishops for one year.

# CHAPTER NINE:

## The Parties to the Battle

The opposition to the Synodal Process is not bashful. Treat the lay people as we always have, simply ignore them, and they'll fall asleep because the majority of Catholics are too lazy and happy enough to remain comfortable with the way things are. That is the "how" and "why" many of the Hierarchy dismiss the Synodal Process.

Cardinals have become accustomed to rejecting those crazy theologians with those gobbledygook ideas about the *sensus fidelium*. Those theologians are just part of those who see the Synodal Process as a way of rabble rousing; nothing but a bunch of disgruntled laity, including those women, who want to run the Church from the pews. That is how some of the Curia are wont to view any attempt at reform. A threat to their power and position is met by a reaction combining fear and disdain.

In some dioceses there has been a passive type of resistance. The listening phase has been treated rather casually, almost ho-hum. Other dioceses simply have not held any formal sessions for listening. Some are scheduled now because the report to the national bishop conferences was released and received publicity in Catholic circles.

Anecdotal evidence captures the atmosphere in many dioceses. Consider the following anecdote: during a session, the Bishop had just outlined the need and plan for parish restructuring because of a shortage of priests. A recent college graduate listened and asked the Bishop, "There are plenty of good Catholic men around, and many women are clamoring to be priests. Why not get more priests from the ranks of the laity? That would eliminate the need to close down or consolidate parishes and upset whole neighborhoods of Catholics." The Bishop stood mute and looked at him as though he was from outer space. He then composed himself and dismissed the suggestion as out of the question. The reaction of the college graduate is quite telling: "Do all of the bishops fall mute when faced with common sense and logic?"

Not all is negative. Several reports tell of the Bishop's sitting down at the card table in the parish gym with the parishioners to assure himself he fully understood every attendee. Over the card table, he could ask questions why the parishioner voiced the complaint or suggestion, but also he could try out his ideas on the lay folk. Further, the presence of the Bishop was noted and gave weight to the pew-Catholics' sentiments.

Pope Francis was explicit in what he hoped the bishops would do and experience. According to Francis, "A synodal church is a listening church, aware that listening is more than hearing. It is a reciprocal listening in which each one has something to learn." Pope Francis likely is very concerned about how little the Bishops and Cardinals have progressed up to now; he wants them to give the process another year.

Talking to the point, Francis observed the following: "The *sensus fidei* makes it impossible to rigidly separate the *ecclesia docens* and the *ecclesia discens* because even the Flock has a 'nose' for discerning the new paths that the Lord is opening up to the church." Sure, the Pope was being positive about the value of views from the pews, but Francis betrays a bit of the Hierarchical attitude when he uses the word "even. " By saying, "*even* the flock," is the Pope surprised that pew-Catholics might have access to the Spirit? Perhaps the Pope was using "even" to emphasize to the Curia that even the pews have the Spirit. However, it could be simply another example of Pope Francis' using poor phrasing. Francis would not have called for the voice from the pews if he did not look for the Holy Spirit among the Faithful.

Ultimately, the Synodal Process will be what the Pope, Cardinals, and Bishops want it to be. Lay persons are no longer able to call a Council or even attend one unless invited by a bishop. The laity originally participated in the Councils; for example, the Synod of Elvira (305AD) and the Synod of Whitby (664AD) included lay members. Vatican I (1869-1870AD), the "Infallibility" Council called by Pius IX, was the first Council without lay members. Then, in the 1917 canons of Church Law, attendance at Councils was officially limited to the ordained. The exception is that bishops may invite "others." One might be led to think that Pope Francis instituted the "listening sessions" precisely to make up for the law of the Church that prohibits lay participants in the Synod.

There are reasons for the pew-Catholic to hope. One reason for hope is Pope Francis has invited lay folks from a variety of backgrounds and professions, some with voting privileges. He also provided a never-before podium to the Faithful at large and instructed the Hierarchy to listen to what the Faithful have to say. In addition, several Bishops from dioceses around the world have made positive statements about key issues raised by the lay Catholics. Vatican II has provided the solid theological foundation of the petitions for reform. Taken together, there is better than a fifty-fifty probability of serious consideration and acceptance of the lay-sponsored reforms.

The reason for the laity to pray is that the track record of the Bishops and Cardinals of the Curia is skewed against change. The status quo is the mantra of the Curia. Traditional Bishops still occupy dioceses.

Many Bishops appointed under the papacies of John Paul II and Benedict XVI are for a strict following of anything Magisterium. Finally, those who opposed the results of the Bishops in the Vatican II Council were stubborn, subtle in some ways, and effective in their opposition; they were able to sabotage most real implementation of the decrees and theology of Vatican II for these past sixty years.

What may be anticipated is the Hierarchy will resist mightily. Simply put, they are asked to give up power, prestige, comfort, privilege, income, and, in some cases, luxury. The Cardinals will see it as a question of who is in control of the Church. On the other hand, the pew-Catholics will see the Synodal Process simply as a chance for a plain recognition of the way things ought to be. Women are children of God just like men, and opening up the priesthood to *probati* or women would solve the priest shortage and cure the need to close parishes. Further, the pew-Catholics, patient with the past foibles of the priests and bishops, will undoubtedly expect action this time on what is perfectly obvious to them.

## Parties to the Battle: The Opposition to Change

*The Curia*

It's no surprise the Cardinals of the Curia choose to oppose the implementation of anything that smacks of the decrees and instructions of the Vatican II Council. Sixty years ago the Cardinals of the Curia opposed the schema of Vatican II. No dummies, they understood immediately the proposal to recognize the sanctity of the conscience of the Child of God reaches right into their offices. For example, if there is no need for an annulment, there is no need for someone in the Curia to review the paperwork and decide to grant an annulment. Vatican II is their stumbling block. Plainly, the Curial power over the souls of believers is diminished. It may be extinguished if the leading moral principle is the sanctity and autonomy of a person's informed conscience as a Child of God. There would be nothing for the Curia to do except to answer questions from those, if any, who have to ask.

A showdown may be unavoidable, and until the postponement by Pope Francis, the showdown was less than a year away. The deciding assembly of the Synod is now scheduled for 2024, but a reading of the issues on the agenda for the Assembly of Bishops can be surmised from a reading of the Report to the National Conferences of Bishops. These reports were in the hands of the Bishops several months before the final working paper, and show a tally of what issues surfaced in the Synodal Process.

These are some of the interests and issues expressed by the laity: concern that priestly sexual abuse not be repeated; how to reverse the decline in attendance at Mass after Covid; what are the proper instructions and disciplines to be exercised on Catholic politicians who adopt positions at odds with Church teaching; it's time, actually overdue, to make women eligible for Holy Orders; stop the public display of disunity between the Pope and Bishops; adopt a more forceful concern for the marginalized—the poor, abused, migrants, LGBTQ+, and disabled.

To cover the details of the contention between the Curia and the proponents of each of these issues is far beyond the scope of this book and is not necessary. The contention in each individual issue boils down to just one question: "Who enjoys the discernment of the Holy Spirit?" It's true each issue presents different mechanics of implementation. But once the decision is made as to who is in charge, what remains is pure mechanics, not theology. That includes even the most fought over issues; admit women to Holy Orders or revise the teaching on homosexuality.

Right from the start, some Cardinals have opposed the conduct of the Synodal Process, and are bright and insightful to understand that whatever the issue, what is to be opposed is the very Synodal Process. Simply to allow the laity to express their ideas of what is needed in the Church is to have lost the battle; that process concedes that the laity enjoy the inspiration of the Holy Spirit. Some Cardinals immediately labeled the Synodal Process "a hostile takeover of the Church." That also sums up the Curia's view: the pews are trying to wrest control of the Church from the Curia. Thus, the battle comes down to who will control and operate the Church, because the battle is over who enjoys the Holy Spirit

*Traditionalist Cardinals*

Pope Francis has stressed the Synodal Process is about "listening to the Holy Spirit," and not about being set in your ways. Pope Francis forewarned the Cardinals of the risk of retreating into the excuse that "We always did it this way."

Of course, it's very natural and universal among humans to abhor change; most folks tend to be set and comfortable with how they have already adapted to the exigencies of their lives. For them, the adjustments have already been made and please don't demand more. Business consultants report a universal response to change in an organization is an old reliable excuse, "But we have always done it this way."

Traditionalist Cardinals have a developed personal network of ideas about how to fulfill their function in the Church. The worldwide clergy has found consultation and even financial support from the Curial offices, which means that they have old established networks, paths with benchmarks along the way in performing their functions. They have mapped out each day of their job, from Monday through Friday. The set of rules, Canon Law and Tradition, have remained unchanged for many years. They developed personal expectations years ago. It doesn't matter that outside circumstances have changed. The Curial offices have their own unchanging circumstances. Consider several years ago there was a very big deal declared when the Curia celebrated finally introducing a computer into the operation of the Annulment Office to speed up the backlog of pending cases.

Up to now, the Curia has never experienced a laity who made a bold challenge to them or acted intrusively on their job performance. Realistically, Curial circumstances and expectations have now changed or will be changing. Now, work life and even personal life may become a challenge. New attitudes need to be developed and that is not easily done at a Cardinal's advanced age. For traditionalists, simply nothing should change.

Specifically, Cardinal Chaput cites the Synodal Process as a danger that could "re-engineer the Church" if the Curia allows it. Cardinal Chaput is joined by Archbishop Philip Tartaglia of Glasgow, who also objects because the "re-engineering'" means "changing." Both Cardinals, enjoying the traditional Hierarchical status, are determined to make sure that nothing changes.

## American Catholic NeoCons

There is a strong Catholic conservative element in the United States. Sometimes that segment of Catholics are referred to as NeoCons. They hold to an unquestioning and strict and literal following of the ten commandments, the commandments of the Church, and every rule and practice of the Church. There is no *epiekeia* in their lexicon. Perhaps the expression of being holier than the Pope describes the movement best. Several U. S. Prelates are numbered in their camp. Author George Weigel in his 2020 book *The Next Pope: The Office Of Peter And A Church In Mission* describes the general flavor of their conservative response to the secular world by posing and answering the question of what is needed in the next Pope. Prelates associated with the NeoCons are definitely opposed to the Pope and the Synodal Process.

Pope Francis did not disabuse the NeoCons of their fear by his off-the-cuff remarks such as when he was asked about homosexuals and replied, "Who am I to judge?" The Pope was speaking to reporters on the Papal plane. The problem is the Pope's casual remark, when reported, causes some to wonder whether the Church will be changing its moral positions. Given their legalistic approach and being of a judgmental mind, the NeoCons will oppose any issue or program they suspect is Pope Francis liberalizing the Church.

Observers have pinpointed their major fear: Pope Francis may decentralize the Church to invoke the principle of subsidiarity. Right now every diocese looks to Rome. Under the principle of subsidiarity, the local Bishop would make decisions based on the local needs and resources of his diocese. The Church would be decentralized. Then, whatever uniformity may have existed will be blown out the Church window. The NeoCons tend toward lockstep religion.

The U.S. Hierarchy in general might be labeled "Neocons" because, being exposed to the realities of a U.S. democratic republic society and its power to the people, they readily realize they will lose their dominant overseer positions upon being required to account for their results to the folks in the pews. It's easier to insist on a set of rules for the people and require strict undifferentiated compliance than abide by the requirements of a shared responsibility.

The origin of the rumor that Pope Francis' retirement or resignation is imminent has been laid at the Neocons' doorstep. The NeoCons offer no comment but aren't unhappy when they consider: Who listens to a lame-duck Pope? On that point, Pope Francis has made known he's in it for the duration.

*Seventy-Four Bishops*

A letter to the German Bishops from seventy-four Cardinals and Bishops opens with, "In an age of rapid global communications, events in one nation inevitably impact ecclesial life elsewhere..." Thus, word had spread among the Catholics of every nation that a boycott had been conducted by the German Catholic women and was answered with a series of synod-like meetings with some members of the German Hierarchy. Word was out that the next meeting of the Germans was to hold a guiding vote on the issues raised and discussed during the four prior meetings; that votes would be cast on matters that seem outside the teaching and practices of the Magisterium.

These seventy-four Prelates warned of what they feared: schism. Perhaps, their intended warning and fear was "SCHISM." Their fear was the German risky meetings would demand an echo in their nations. They worried internationally, representing the continents of Africa,

Australia, North America, and Europe. The warning carried the weight
of prominent and influential Prelates: U.S. Cardinal Raymond Burke,
Australian Cardinal George Pell, and Nigerian Cardinal Francis Arinze.
Their concern also tells of how the world has shrunk into a
neighborhood.

Their fear may have originated with remarks of German Bishop Georg
Batzing, then President of the German Bishop Conference. The specific
instance was that of Bishop Batzing's response to criticism from the
Curia. He offered a theological assertion of administrative
independence. First, Batzing indicated his German Catholics had
definitely received the Holy Spirit. He then raised the question: Why
should his German Catholics have to wait to act upon their inspirations
from the Holy Spirit until the rest of the Catholic world caught up to
them?

The Curia's answer was that uniformity and homogeneity in doctrine
and practice are to be preserved. Bishop Batzing rejected this reply.
The Bishop considered uniformity an excuse for non-action. Batzing
made it clear that uniformity is not unity; he did not consider uniformity
a sufficient reason for the German Catholics to wait. Bishop Batzing's
remark was considered something of a threat, even though Batzing had
stated clearly and on several occasions that schism was never on his
mind. Finally, in their warning to the German Bishops, these seventy-
four Bishops telegraphed how they would vote in the coming Assembly
of Bishops.

*Vocation-Driven Cardinals*

Some young men join the seminary with less than totally spiritual
motivations. However, what is quite surprising are the seminarians who

enter the training for the Catholic priesthood with a specific pontifical position in mind. Their ambition is readily apparent and quite specific; they arrive with Bishop Miters packed in their luggage. One seminarian came with a full steamer trunk packed with the regalia of a Cardinal. Amazingly, all this was placed into their luggage before they left home. Oversized ambition in a Church setting seems totally unbecoming but nevertheless it exists and leads an observer to guess these prelates are not going to vote away their honor, power, or luxury.

## Assessment of the Opposition to Reform

Pope Francis will go forward with the Council and will take up what is proposed by the Faithful. Those proposals will be opposed by the Prelates who echo the thought of the late Cardinals Pell of Australia and active Cardinal Muller of Germany who asserted, "Dismiss the synodal process, only clergy own discernment and decide." Those Prelates have been quite open in their opposition to Pope Francis and the Synodal Process. They are reported to have taken up residence in a Rome apartment to "work the room," as it's said in politics. They stationed themselves strategically. Rome is where Cardinals and Bishops come eventually. Even with the death of Cardinal Pell, their original purpose remains, to meet with Prelates and to persuade them to vote against the Synodal process and any of its proposals.

That prompts the question: is politicking appropriate in the affairs of the Church? The answer appears to be this: the Church is an institution of men on earth. The outcome of the Synodal Process is in the hands of men on earth who will operate how people tend to operate in a society. That is both an obstacle and an opportunity for the Spirit. It is an obstacle because the Holy Spirit usually works through nature. But it is an opportunity because the Holy Spirit usually works through nature. Definitely the Holy Spirit knows politics too. .

Politics in a Church setting causes one to pause, but the Holy Spirit is involved here by way of inspiration of the parties involved. Think of an elevator cabin. Two associates are riding the elevator; it stops and another person joins the ride up. Upon the elevator's resumption, the passenger composition and atmosphere of the cabin changed; at that time an unspoken, almost electric, dynamic change occurs among the passengers; the original two associates might change both content and tone of their conversation. The person joining the two associates might adopt a posture of isolation or of smiling community. Even an elevator cabin shows results of a silent electric dynamic: nervousness, feigned friendliness, rigid formality, etc. The point is the Holy Spirit might end up riding the elevator with some of the currently-opposed Curial Bishops and Cardinals.

## Parties to the Battle Proposing Change

### German Hierarchy

The initial major engagement between the pews and the pulpits started in the major cities of Germany. The Catholic women boycotted. Several German Bishops listened; they avoided getting angry. That listening made a difference! The three Catholic German women's organizations joined by the overarching German Catholic association were invited to visit with the German Hierarchy in synodal-like format. Cardinal Marx desired to keep a very open flow of ideas and felt the formal synod format stymied the free flow of the desired conversation. Based on the results thus far, the synodal-like meetings have been open with honest opinions and it seems very cordial.

One result of the German Catholic meetings, perhaps noted by the Vatican and in dioceses worldwide, was an approval to rethink the moral theology covering homosexuality. When the preliminary vote was counted, forty, more than a majority, of the Prelates voted for rethinking the issue of gender sexuality. Eight Prelates voted against the proposal.

The original subject of protest, women's being excluded from the administration and worship of the Church, was also addressed. The preliminary vote on the proposition that women be deacons was approved by 93% of all delegates. The vote of just the Bishops tallied 45 (82 %) voting "Aye," and 10 (18 %) voting "Nay." The lack of a one-hundred-percent vote for or against is an indicator there was no railroading of anyone. The Prelates were respectful of one another's thinking and prejudices.

Another meeting is scheduled. The Bishops and the German Catholics will meet to cast votes on more proposals. The proposals represent work done in concert, issues from the pews and issues from the pulpit. Cardinal Gerhard Marx deserves the credit for bringing the Hierarchy together, managing the Curia in Rome and conservative critic Cardinal Woelki in Cologne.

The leading German Catholic conservative, Cardinal Woelki, opposed the German meetings and signaled opposition to the Synodal Process right from the start. Cardinal Woelki has problems of his own, failing to release the reports of an outside audit of priestly sexual-abuse cases in his diocese. His hiding the report caused a loss of trust across the entire German Hierarchy.

That lack of trust also produced sad outcomes: 359,338 Catholics left the Church in 2021. In 2020, as many as 221,390 closed the door on the Church. The numbers suggest a quiet de facto schism is taking place in Germany. The question is whether the Synodal Process will reverse the erosion of membership.

*The American Bishops*

As noted before, the American episcopate tends Neocon. But Cardinals and Bishops known to be aligned with Pope Francis are Cardinal Cupich of the Archdiocese of Chicago, San Diego Bishop Robert McElroy, now elevated to Cardinal by Pope Francis, and in Indianapolis Cardinal Joseph William Tobin speaks of ways "to engage" sinners and the marginalized.

The other major-city Cardinals and Archbishops have been operating close to the vest. One observer suggests the American Prelates are more likely to vote against the pew-sponsored reforms because of their general opposition to Pope Francis. Questions have been raised. Did New York's Cardinal Dolan set a rather elaborate set of instructions for the conduct of the listening sessions as a subtle discouragement to would-be participants?

*United Kingdom and the Continents*

Recently rocked by a horrible sexual-abuse scandal, the Irish Prelates are very much in the spotlight. Archbishop of Dublin, Dermot Farrell, noted the decrease in priestly vocations against the approaching retirement age of his elderly priests. He noted his visit with Pope Francis centered around discernment of the Spirit. His independent observation is about "certain reform that is somewhat overdue." With discernment and discerned reform on his mind, Archbishop Farrell and his fellow bishops can likely be labeled an "Aye" on reform issues.

In England over the past ten years, there has been a movement for a change in the mandatory celibacy requirement for priests. This movement has been aroused by the Catholic Church itself. The acceptance and re-ordination of married Anglican priests into Catholic dioceses and parishes has called attention to certain benefits of married clergy. The Catholic bishops have noticed the benefits.

In an interview with *The Tablet,* the British Bishops, Seamus Cunningham, Tom Burns, and Thomas McMahon recounted their experience with married priests (ex-Anglican priests who have been assigned to their dioceses). Their support for a married priesthood is clear. Bishop McMahon has indicated that he thinks people in those parishes where [married priests] have been placed have taken to them very well. His key observation is that good ministry is what matters and the marital status of the priest is secondary. These British Bishops may be guessed to back an expansion of the priesthood.

Bishop Cunningham leans toward the possibility of *probati* to the priesthood. His spokesperson elaborates the *probati* would help overcome the difficulties resulting from the shortage of priests. That would ring a sympathetic chord in the U. S., where many Catholics have seen their Church mothballed and their Sunday Mass now fifteen miles farther away.

Among the English Hierarchy, the pew-sponsored proposals for reform appear positive. Reports are that Cardinal Vincent Nichols, President of the Bishops Conference of England and Wales, has stressed the listening aspect of the Synodal Process. The Cardinal, inviting the

Faithful's views, speaks of their importance in the discernment process by declaring we seem to become creative when we respond to the call of Jesus. That is a move away from the *status quo*. It seems Cardinal Nichols was an advocate of the Synodal Process from the very start.

Turning to Europe, in Milan, how much of the legacy of the Jesuit Cardinal Carlo Maria Montini remains will influence the Northern Italy vote. Cardinal Josef Deresel of Brussels is known for his liberal stance. In Spain, Cardinal Osoro Sierra of Madrid is among the more liberal Cardinals elevated by Pope Francis.

As to Africa, Cardinal Mario Zenari represents a liberal bent in Syria and Cardinal Dieudonne Nzapalawga is known for definite progressive stances in the Central Africa Republic. Trying to sum the Continent's stance is risky, but those clerics and lay folks seem to have clearly exhibited a very strong sentiment for liberating the Church from European trappings and opening the Church to what has become known as inculturation; let them express the gospel truths in their African way of life. That might signal regular "Aye's."

**Assessment of Those for Reform**

The Cardinals and Bishops who lean toward a more "Vatican II Church" are scattered throughout the world-Church. Those opposed to Vatican II tend to be concentrated in and around the Curia in Rome. But distance from Rome allows only a sketchy picture of where the ultimate vote of the outlying Bishops will take the Church. However, it appears there are enough Bishops who will advocate and vote for a "Vatican II Church," and that would certainly make the Assembly of Bishops a great television program if that ever were to be permitted.

## The Ultimate Party to the Battle: the Holy Spirit

The key party to determine the outcome of the Synodal Process has yet to be noted: the Holy Spirit is Jesus' Promise. In all these considerations, the ultimate party to determine the outcome of the Assembly of Bishops is the Holy Spirit. But the theological paradox is that the *divine operates through the human.* The Paraclete has to do it through a society of men, an institution of men. That is why discussion is valuable: assessing what the Holy Spirit has to work with will cause us even more wonder upon the outcome. What, where, how, when, and if the Holy Spirit will intervene will and must nevertheless come through an institution of men.

# CHAPTER TEN:

## The Ultimate Battlefield and Solution for the Problems of the Church

The Council of Vatican II ended with the Church experiencing joy and hope in the pews. There were smiles on most Catholic faces. When had the pulpit ever before spoken of "freedom" of conscience? They and their non-Catholic buddies need not feel uncomfortable in each other's presence anymore. Each could have a different opinion about whether Mary was assumed bodily into heaven without feeling a discounted opinion of one for the other. Post Vatican II, most Catholics were tickled at the mention of Pope John XXIII, who when asked how many people worked at the Vatican replied, "About half of them." Most were proud of their Church; most liked the new vernacular Sunday Mass and saw it as a sign of even better things to come. Catholics were anticipating still more good things to come of Vatican II.

That was not the atmosphere in the corridors of the Curia, however. Also, during Vatican II in the debates over the schema, there were negative votes. Those negative votes had been cast by very hard-line prelates who would oppose any change to their status quo. Vatican Curia Cardinals and Bishops had decided to dig in their heels. Those prelates desired to put a stop to all that change; those prelates were led by soon-to-be Popes John Paul II and Benedict XVI.

The Curia and Bishops governing the Church were not prepared for an engaged laity. The layer of inertial years in which the Pope was God and the Cardinals and Bishops sat next to God did not prepare the Curia and the Hierarchy for a seriously active Faithful. Given recognized dignity as a child of God, the pew Catholic was prepared to exercise his freedom of conscience. As it turned out, Cardinal Ratzinger, head of the Congregation for the Faith, was unwilling to allow Catholics to use their own lights to navigate life. The Congregation, in the person of Cardinal Ratzinger, decided Catholics, no matter what their heads tell them, are to obey the teaching and ruling of the Magisterium. That was ironic. Everyone in the world had just been granted freedom of conscience—except Catholics, whose Church just granted freedom of conscience to everyone in the world. How does that square? The Vatican just could not accept the idea of their members being responsible for their own actions.

The times continued dynamic. An estimate from the 1970s was that the world's knowledge was doubling every five years. The space race led to systems that commercialized inventions in less than five years. It used to take as much as fifteen to twenty years when economist Schumpeter offered his business-cycle theory of entrepreneurship as the driver of national economies. Products were becoming obsolete as soon as they became popular.

The Vatican marched in place, not really engaging the world, censuring theologians who offered ways to reach into the places where people actually lived. The Vatican created a whole class of Catholics who adjusted their lives by their consciences, whom the Prelates recognized as the "Cafeteria Catholics." The Church maintained an appearance of relevancy by fostering a Papal personality cult—the Pope John Paul II Road Show. In stadium after stadium, youth gathered to see a Pope who was squelching theological studies addressing the practical morality of their future lives. And worse, the Vatican was pushing a Pope as the "Patron of Youth" who, when those youth entered their late thirties, would be found to be an enabler of priests' pedophilia. This is how the

Catholic Church continued after Vatican II in its status quo—alongside but never engaged with the unclean world it was meant to renew.

## The Gift of Prophesy

No one knows the future, of course. But incidents of prophesy appear in the Scriptures. The art of prophesy is not really about having a special vision from the Archangel Gabriel. Prophesy is at the same time much simpler and much harder than an Archangel's visit. Prophesy is a paradox: *prophesy is the capacity of a person to understand the present.* By drilling down into the innermost workings of the present situation, by understanding the various forces influencing the main characters and weighing the gravity of possible outcomes, the prophet sees the natural consequences of the current forces, trends, influences, characters, and feasibilities of the present situation.

An apt analogy may be drawn from the science of physics. If you have a ball of known weight and circumference in the middle of an almost frictionless road with a slope of six degrees to the west and a wind blowing from the north at twenty-one miles per hour, the physicist will tell you the direction of the combined torque of the wind and slope will take the ball. Likewise, taking into account what is known about the battlefields (the issues) and the parties (the Pope, Cardinals, Bishops, theologians, and lay advocates), the prophet may tell you what the Church might look like after the Synodal Process.

Nonetheless, there is one variable that remains unknown until it shows itself. What is not known is the how or when the Holy Spirit will decide to operate. Miracles can happen when the Holy Spirit whispers to the parties—and if the parties are open to the Spirit. In any case, the Spirit is still having to deal with an institution of men. If any prophesy seems appropriate here, it is that there will be a battle of bishops, those for the status quo opposed to those intent on becoming.

## *Resolution Step One:*
## *Recognize the Extent of the Universal Priesthood*

In business, one of the problem-solving techniques is the process called "brainstorming." The brainstorming process begins with invitations to a meeting. All the staff who are directly involved in the problem area (and also folks from related areas) are invited. Once gathered, the group is instructed to speak—even shout out—whatever comes to mind that might solve a certain problem. No judgment or evaluation of suggestions is allowed at this juncture; just suggestions of whatever comes to mind.. As the participants say their ideas, a person (or persons) serves as recorder(s) at the chalk board(s) or flip chart(s), recording the responses. The idea is registered as close to a quote as possible to capture the flavor of the suggestion. Usually the process ends upon the natural exhaustion of ideas from the group.

Next, each suggestion by suggestion is examined to cast it into a format that fits the situation or to clarify its use within the business. The attitude is *"How can we make this work?"* Judgment or evaluation as to how well it might work is still avoided at this point.

However, once the suggestions have been made into "meanings," or "actionable statements," the moderator leads the discussion of each as a practical application to the problem and its likelihood of success. In general, the attitude is to try to make the suggestion work somehow. Then the session closes by ranking the group's estimate of probability they attach to each suggestion. The idea is to end with a ranked set of solutions that constitute a general strategy and a program to solve the problem.

## Brainstorming the Universal Priesthood of the People of God

No matter how the Synodal Process will end, the office of priest will remain. Besides its tradition in the Bible, Catholic theology has elaborated the sacramentality of a priest's major function to serve as God's witness through the People of God in this world. For example, the priest witnesses the outpouring of God's love upon us as we solemnize special events in our lives. We solemnize and celebrate our creation and kinship to God in the Sacrament of Baptism; we solemnize and celebrate God's intimacy with us in the Eucharist; we solemnize and celebrate our choice of a life partner, while the priest witnesses God's blessing upon us as we rejoice at becoming one. In Holy Orders, the Bishop witnesses God's grace upon a soul solemnizing and celebrating his dedication to God's formal worship and service of Jesus' followers. Our major transitions in life have God's love witnessed by the presence of the priest. We label these Sacraments; they are the outward sign of God's blessing on our major life passages. We label these life-passage witnessings Sacraments with a big "S."

God does not take time off between our special life occasions, however. God bothers with us every day, every hour, every moment of our lives. We become witnesses to God's presence every moment in our lives and our world. For example, as an instrument of God's care in the everyday, we share our homemade ham and bean soup with the elderly neighbor lady living alone. We bring something good into her life. It's how we witness to God's reach into her life. Often, folks will say, "God bless you," recognizing that all good comes from God. We also witness to

God's goodness and love in the everyday. Those acts are sacramental, too. They are sacraments with a little "s."

The little "s" sacraments are some of the ways we partake in the universal priesthood of the People of God. *The universal priesthood is the vehicle we use to work for the Kingdom in an unclean world.* Our lives present many opportunities every day to share in the priesthood of Jesus. After all, the gospel accounts tell us of Jesus' "going about doing good." We can do the same but there is another significant option within the universal priesthood of the People of God that the Church does not emphasize.

This option is generally unknown and mostly forgotten. It completes the charisms of Baptism for the Jesus follower. The Bishops of the Council of Trent, in their consideration of the big "S" Sacraments, decreed *the performing the outward sign of the Sacrament is what calls God and his power into our souls.* The power of the Sacrament is in the performance of the outward sign. Indeed, this is the emphasis of the Council of Trent: *it is not the "ordained-ness" of the priest* that causes the blessing of God to come upon us. It is the performance of the outward sign!

Why would the Council of Trent make a rule about what makes a Sacrament a Sacrament? Back then the Faithful worried and wanted a clarification: does a person receive the benefit of the sacraments if an unworthy priest performs the sacrament? For example, "If the priest is in mortal sin, are my sins forgiven?" The answer of the Bishops of Trent was a Sacrament is valid because the benefit of the Sacrament does **not** derive from *ex opere operantis* (i.e., "the presence and act of the **performer**"). Instead, the Bishops of Trent decreed the efficacy of the Sacrament stems from *ex opere operandum*: from the "**performance** of the outward sign." It is the pouring of the water, the exchange of vows by the bride and groom, the words and intent of consecration of the bread and wine—that is what brings God into our world. It is not the priest's ordained-ness!

The early followers of Jesus were the first to witness to Jesus. In Acts, Peter's Pentecost talk to those gathered says explicitly that "We are witness to Jesus." Then they started the formal witness by holding a memorial meal in honor of Jesus. Church history tells us about the presiders who first lead the Jesus memorial meal. The presiders were usually the heads of the household where the meal was being held. The presiders served as the chief witnesses to the memory of Jesus. After all were gathered at the table, the presider spoke of his or her encounter with Jesus. Then, all at the meal would in turn recall their encounters with Jesus. They would recount conversations they had with Jesus or perhaps a healing they received from him. These gatherings were not unlike our post-funeral lunches, where those attending are curious about how the other person came to know the deceased. Also, the Jesus memorial meal was not unlike our Mass, except instead of a priest, a senior family member conducted the order of memories and arranged for memorializing Jesus in the sharing of the bread and wine.

When it came time to memorialize Jesus in partaking of the bread and the wine, the presider called attention to the solemnity of remembering Jesus, and with that petitioned the Father to grant the bread and the wine to become their Jesus-spiritual-nourishment, reciting the words of consecration as remembered in the Jesus tradition. Furthermore, the celebration of Jesus' memory became real, and those assembled in the home witnessed the Jesus-embodiment of the bread and wine. There were no Holy Orders; there were no ordained; there were only Jesus followers, simply engaged in remembering—better yet—memorializing Jesus.

We note the Hebrew word "to remember" was for the Jewish people a very rich word—to remember was not simply an idea in the mind. but a reassembly of the reality; the deceased did not simply come to mind, but became real, present, and alive to the person. To remember was to make it real here and now. When the early Jesus followers "remembered" Jesus, they were making Jesus real again for them there and then. From that we may understand the experience of the early followers of Jesus as memorial leaders and the Council of Trent's sacramental decree to establish the Universal Priesthood. The idea of the Universal Priesthood comes from a fuller understanding of the charisms bestowed in Baptism. (Of course, this is the precise basis for the Catholic women to establish the theological foundation for their admittance to the priesthood.)

Under the Universal Priesthood of the Faithful, the formally ordained continue their roles and their importance. The ordained priest becomes the formal delegate of the People of God. The person designated presides as the people's formal witness in the exercise of the Sacraments, with the big "S." For many and obvious reasons the entire body of Jesus followers cannot be present to witness each Baptism or Wedding. By delegation, the ordained step in as the entire community of God's people to witness to the conduct of each Sacrament. The delegation occurs, as described in the Gospel, by the Faithful's "laying on of hands," and the person-delegate accepts the role of ordained and its dedication to the service of the servants of God.

## Everyone's a Priest

The Council of Trent made it possible that the entire priesthood is open to the pew-Catholic. The Bishops of the Council of Trent were quite explicit: the Sacrament's effect derives from performance of the ritual; and Trent was clear, calling it heresy to hold *ex opere operantis, because of the performer.* *We* acknowledge the benefit of the Sacrament comes from the act that is performed, the symbol of God's operation in our world. If placed alongside the fact the entire priesthood is open to the pew-Catholic and if full participation in the Church is expected of the Child of God, then the conclusion becomes that everyone is a priest with a capital "P."

Almost every Catholic will be surprised to think of oneself as a Priest. But the history of the early followers of Jesus in the era of the "Home Church" testify to the official priesthood of the individual believer, both men and women. That point is not regularly brought forward. The simplicity of how the early followers participated in the Church is fascinating. Persecution, early on, meant whispering and meeting in secret to witness. Later, with the worry about Roman search and persecution no longer needed, the followers of Jesus could arrange services among themselves: "Who will host our memorial meal tonight? Will the head of the household preside or should someone else? What time should we meet?" If a Jesus follower from 40 AD were to appear now, that person would be surprised at the compartmentalizing of our Church. Indeed, early Jesus followers would feel right at home with the idea of everyone's being a Priest. His or her reaction might be, "What's the big deal?"

## The Kingdom of God in an Unclean World

Every day most Catholics perform a sacrament with a little "s," and thereby witness to Jesus by bringing some good to another. The little "s" is part of the Universal Priesthood. You shovel the walk of an elderly couple; you are patient with your spouse on a "really bad day;" you visit a friend in town because her children do not live nearby. What you've done is to bring some goodness, some love, and some of God's love into our world.

The performance of the little "s" sacraments are a basic way of establishing the Kingdom of God in our unclean world. The Universal Priesthood of the People of God is to "sacramentize" the world, to make holy the world; to witness to the world that Goodness, that God-ness reigns, and to wear away at the unclean world. The role of universal priesthood is important in carrying out Jesus' instruction to work for the Kingdom; the little "s" sacraments are handy for the priesthood all day and every day.

Not to be forgotten are two points. First, the formal priesthood and the big "S" Sacraments (what we now associate only with the ordained) were granted by the Council of Trent to all believers. Second, *Gaudium et Spes,* decree of Vatican II, calls the pew-Catholics to a deeper devotion and fuller participation in the Church. Taken together, being a priest of and full participation in the Church means that the pew-Catholic may no longer simply look up at the altar from the pew as a spectator. The pew-Catholic must be intent upon and consciously join in the memorializing of Jesus; must join the presider in saying the words of consecration over the bread and wine. And the presider, by the way, no longer may see how quickly he can "get through" a Mass. Now the presider—aware of the pews where his co-celebrators of the

Eucharist wait—is to be aware of and sure to include the pews in the Eucharist. Turned toward the pews, under the Vatican II directive, the priest calls the pew-Catholic's attention to the solemnity of the moment, asks the pews to remember Jesus, and invites the pews to join in the consecration of the bread and wine. The entire congregation joins in reciting the words of institution and then communes and celebrates with Jesus. The memorializing of Jesus brings Jesus among the People of God on their journey to the Kingdom, extending Jesus in time and space.

## The Office of the Priest

Actually, it is not totally new to associate the priesthood with the laity. This is especially true when you consider the Church has elevated to the priesthood and the office of Bishop not only a lay person, but someone who wasn't even Catholic when made Bishop! That was St. Ambrose.

While serving as the Emperor's Representative to Milan, Ambrose was asked to settle a dispute between two local Church factions. Those factions were at odds over who the next Bishop of Milan should be. As Ambrose worked with these warring parties, they each saw in Ambrose his talent, especially his fairness, and wisdom; the next thing, both parties decided Ambrose should be their next bishop! Ambrose, not a Catholic, said "No," and quickly fled from the city. Before you knew it, the citizens contacted the Emperor and he gave a command ordering Ambrose to return to Milan. After an eight-day short course on theology and the duties of a bishop, the Catholics of Milan "laid hands on" Ambrose; thus, consecrating him the Bishop of Milan. Knowing of the universal priesthood and learning of the experience of Ambrose, this question presents itself: What really is the formal office of priest? Who can be expected to serve as priest?

The office of priest is that of a delegate of the People before God. It covers the formal, official, and communal relations of the People to God in contrast to individual private prayer and adoration. By "the laying on of hands," the pew-Catholics delegate their communal official duties to the "ordained." The "ordained" is thereby commissioned to serve as representative of the community of believers before God. The commission of the Priest as delegate involves nothing unusual, but rather what God expects of his people: humble adoration, contrite confession, sincere thanksgiving, and childlike supplication.

Jesus was limited in space and time in his mission to make the world holy according to his Father's intent. The task then falls to Jesus' followers in history. Not everyone can be present to all the needs; therefore, the priest becomes the official delegate of the entire community to carry on Jesus' mission. As a rule the priest is delegated the big "S" Sacraments. At the same time, having delegated the official witness to the ordained does not mean to limit the pew-Catholics to the little "s" sacraments. Perhaps eventually decentralization will allow all Jesus followers the exercise of the full priesthood in their individual lives.

**Decentralization and Universal Priesthood**

The principle of decentralization is especially applicable to an organization that finds itself with branches in various environments, cultures, and life tempos. German Bishop Batzing has been quite definite in pointing to his diocese's need for decentralization from Rome. The Bishop quite frankly told of how his people are ahead of others in having received the Spirit's inspiration regarding women's Holy Orders, charity toward homosexuals, solving the priest shortage, and going a long way to stop the exodus of the distressed Catholics. The only reasons the Vatican offers for Bishop Batzing to hold off is to maintain general conformity and a desired homogeneity throughout the Church. Batzing is not convinced of the need to have everyone conform to the same program; Batzing recognizes uniformity is not unity. Other bishops agree with him and certainly the members of his diocese also agree.

It is obvious the dioceses on one side of the globe are significantly different from those on the other. Even within the continents, dioceses exhibit differences in life tempos, environments, and cultures. That argues for the possibility of different gifts in each different diocese. For example, Pope Francis entertained the culture of the Amazon at the Vatican's religious services in recognition of such differences in the Church. The Spirit works through nature—through the natural process of life and our humanity. The Spirit will not and cannot be expected to ignore or overturn what the Creator Father established in his act of Creation. The Spirit operates through and builds on nature. Therefore, the observation of Bishop Batzing that his diocese should not have to wait for the rest of the dioceses in the world to catch up to his diocese is perfectly logical, well founded in theology and nature, and follows a sound principle of organizational theory—namely, decentralization.

This reasoning applies to the entire list of gifts of the Holy Spirit. It allows the pew-Catholic to exercise the full gamut of mission in their everyday lives. Yes, the community does need the priest as the formal and official representative of the community. The entire community would still gather for the official worship of God. Whatever the case may be, this does not preclude the pew-Catholics from exercising their privilege of the Universal Priesthood, presiding at a Jesus memorial meal in their family or neighborhood setting, which harkens back to the days of the "home churches." Families all around the world might also decide to meet in a memorial of Jesus; the Eucharist is licit and valid under the decree of Trent, the theology of the Spirit's respect for its own creation, and the obvious differences in life tempos, environments, and cultures in diocesan makeup.

Consider the following example of how the privilege of the priesthood might work: The head of the household together with spouse and other family members determine the night before what time the next day's main meal will be. All understand the main meal will be the Jesus memorial meal. Members are welcome to invite others to the memorial. The next day, at the appointed time, the head of the household gathers the family around the dinner table, welcomes them, and invites them each to recount a blessing received of Jesus. The head of the household or whoever is serving as presider asks those present to offer themselves to the Father before proceeding to the co-consecration of the bread and wine. The family performs the consecration together and then partakes; the memorial ends with all present giving thanks as a group or individually.

## *Resolution Step Two:*
## *Decentralize the Gifts of the Holy Spirit*

There is irony in the Hierarchy's denial of the Spirit to the Faithful. Actually, it was the Hierarchy, in the persons of the Fathers of the Church, who defined the doctrine of the Church after they picked the minds of the early believers in Jesus. They got the doctrine from the Faithful but now they won't let the Faithful interpret or amend their own doctrine.

It is like this: The Fathers of the Church, a long time ago, were trying to codify what the Faithful were thinking and doing. Typical were Augustine, Gregory of Nazianzus, and John Chrysostom who were all practicing theology in trying to codify the living Faith of the early Jesus followers. That determined what came to be Church doctrine. They did that based on what the early followers of Jesus were doing and praying. Today's Church doctrine is a codification of what the Fathers of the Church heard and saw. Accordingly, present-day pew-Catholics know only that Church doctrine is somehow tied in with the early church and the Fathers of the Church, but the work of those Fathers needs to be understood as an attempt to generalize the personal and rationalize the dynamic as exhibited by the early Jesus followers. *But trying to apply to everyone what's personal to the early followers and to freeze what's dynamic falls short of doing either.*

In addition, the Fathers used in their analysis the backdrop of the culture, norms, and ideology of their time. St. Augustine is a great example: his deep fear of sinful concupiscence was his reaction to his life environment and his times. He was limited to the tradition that only saw Jesus as a sacrificial lamb. Therefore, what the Church teaches today is a doctrine that's a museum piece. The Hierarchy are curators of the Fathers' work. Their thought persists and nothing more need be found or decided. The problem is humans are alive; people live in a dynamic history. And so does God. People continue to learn and to grow but the Hierarchy froze the theology from the Fathers.

The Fathers held to certain presuppositions of theology that over time have proved to be false. An example is how today's economy operates by relying heavily on lines of credit. Loans and interest are in almost everyone's life. At one point, however, the Church declared charging interest on loaned funds is a sin. The presupposition was that money was inertial. The Hierarchy did not understand or appreciate money's use in multiple environments and purposes—the fungibility of money.

The point is the Hierarchy of today operates on the past. They operate as though everything that could possibly be revealed has been revealed. To accept their premise, a person has to ignore all the advances made in our knowledge of ourselves. How Augustine understood human motivation is not the present day understanding of what motivates us. Simply, the multiplicity of just the external influences that stimulate us every day compared to that of Augustine's time has no comparison. The question is this: Why did the Hierarchy think and act as though the Holy Spirit has retired and left the building? It's to maintain the status quo.

**The Loss of Pluralism**

The Church destroyed the beauty of its pluralism when the Hierarchy insisted on controlling the *sensus fidelium* by mandating a homogeneous doctrine and practice. The reflection of Jesus from the people of different cultures and lands disappeared. The cookie-cutter Church and believer took its place.

The early Jesus communities, each with its remembrance of Jesus, were diverse and unique, and that is the whole point: the *sensus fidelium* of the early Jesus followers did not fit into a single sophisticated statement; it was a hodgepodge of plain remembrances of a Jesus talking to or eating with the villagers. It's fair to say two people in the same encounter with Jesus may each have come away with something that struck them differently. They would offer different accounts based on their backgrounds. Nevertheless, the Fathers of the Church, later the Hierarchy, forced what was a personal expression of a peasant into a sophisticated proposition. As theoreticians, they did it in excruciating detail. The Fathers tried bottling up the Spirit. The congregation for the Faith insists everyone must be in lockstep, with even the exact same words of expression. In turn, the congregation has destroyed the creativity of the Jesus follower, the different ways to contemplate, love, and follow Jesus.

## Jesus is the Doctrine, the Norm, the Measure of Morals

The Church spends energy keeping a set of books but overlooks what is right out in the open: Jesus said, "I am the way." Simply, in all human activity Jesus is the norm, the doctrine, the ethic, the moral principle, and the North Star. Originally, God gave Moses the norm in the Ten Commandments. The stiff-necked tribe of David had the rules for how they should live. But when it came to the second time? God gave us a person, Jesus, the norm, doctrine, ethic, moral principle, and North Star. The world has the rules on how to live in the person of Jesus.

If you were among those who met Jesus, you would have a firsthand idea of how he conducted himself, how he talked, how he revealed his priorities and values. You would have seen how he came across to you and your friends. His presence and interplay with you and others would reveal how to live life. When Jesus visited with folks in the villages, he impressed them. Some decided to imitate Jesus, the way he treated others, how he carried himself, how he welcomed even the lower caste, ate with whoever wanted to dine with him, and exuded a love of God.

One village, known as the *Diddache* community, actually wrote a set of instructions after being visited by Jesus. In fact, Jesus' presence was so strong, one instruction in the *Diddache* manual actually tells the villagers simply to remember how Jesus conducted himself.[1] The point is that those who saw Jesus understood he was the way to life, was someone to follow, was a norm worthy of their energy and imitation. That was the power of his presence.

## The Fathers of the Church and Doctrine

When the Fathers of the Church came on the scene, they tried to formulate doctrine from the people who had met Jesus. The Fathers (of an intellectual bent) wanted to understand and make sense of what those early followers of Jesus believed and how they behaved. Hence, they set out to rationalize what is spontaneously personal, and to generalize what is totally specific. No two people responded to Jesus exactly the same because they are two different people.

The Fathers knew the early followers of Jesus honored Jesus; they held a memorial meal in honor of Jesus. That is natural; we do the same for our deceased friends and heroes. You can't rationalize what is natural and spontaneous. If you do, you supply something, a framework, a thesis, a principle of some kind.. That's exactly what the Fathers did in writing doctrine from their observations of the early Church.

To further explain this, take a look at the following example of Augustine trying to solve what bothered the minds of the Fathers: Why do we sin? Are we totally bad? No. Are we totally good? No. So why do we sin?

St. Augustine provided an answer by supplying a framework; thus, he "invented" Original Sin. Augustine avoided having to say that we're all

---

[1] That instruction had to do with how to determine who is a genuine itinerant preacher as opposed to some religious hustler.

good or all bad. He placed the answer outside of the individual person. Original Sin—Adam's sin—so weakened us that we are prone to sin. Augustine made up another answer when asked how exactly is Original Sin transmitted from one generation to succeeding generations: his answer was it is transmitted through the man's penis!

Augustine and the other Fathers of the Church supplied their framework to determine what Jesus meant to his early followers. The current Hierarchy still look to the Fathers of the Church for the foundation of today's doctrine that arose out of the intellects and imaginations of the Fathers of the Church. They tried to understand and explain how and why the early followers of Jesus did what they did, but supplied their own framework in doing so.

The point: The early followers of Jesus memorialized Jesus based on their individual inspirations of the Holy Spirit. The Church tried to capture what the early followers did but ended in supplying their framework from their ideologies and prejudices. What is needed is a way to restore the original memorializing of Jesus, to decentralize the Church doctrine.

## *Resolution Step Three:*
## *Pope Francis Defines the Common Understanding*

Will Pope Francis be able to find a resolution between the entrenched "Nays" and the pressing "Ayes"? The "Nays" seem to fix on the status quo and belittle the proposals for change as a power grab. The "Ayes" seem to fix on the inadequacies, even sinfulness, of existing Church operation. New science-based presuppositions are offered for revised theological formulations. The new theological insights offer a new way to view Church practices. It is a case of the status quo versus possibilities.

One avenue for Pope Francis is to follow the framework from the studies of Jesuit Fr. John Courtney Murray. Pope Francis might focus on how a state (the U.S., or in this case, the Church) might accommodate a divergence (Plural Political Parties, or in this case, Plural Theologies). Pope Francis faces a Church with its current norms (kept by the Curia) and the question of how to allow accommodation of possible divergences (reform theologies and behaviors) from the norms (the Magisterium) within the Church.

Fr. Murray, based on his study of plurality in the United Stares, suggests a method for accommodating plurality in a society: Every legitimate apparent divergence has to fall within the bounds of a common understanding; by definition, a divergence implies a norm from which to diverge; that divergence must not offend what people hold as a set of common values. In the case of the United States, Fr. Murray found the boundaries were the general acceptance of the Judeo-Christian ethic. That defined the bounds within which a divergence could fall and not be considered extreme or unpatriotic.

The Church has a defined set of values and ethics. For the sake of exposition let's define the set as the life of Jesus, the Great Commandment, the Ten Commandments, and the Nicaean Creed. The life of Jesus tells us a great deal of what is Jesus-like and what is not. Jesus himself is reported in the gospel as offering the Great Commandment as our North Star. The Ten Commandments were certainly within the Jewish tradition. The Bishops at the Council of Nicaea adopted the Creed we recite at each Sunday Mass. Therefore, consider the following as a step to a possible solution: Pope Francis could establish the Ten Commandments, the Great Commandment, and the Creed as the common field.

Then, if a proposal falls within the common field, the next test is assigned to the Assembly of Bishops. The Bishops in the Council must agree that the divergence falls within what they consider Jesus-like. If the Bishops do not find the proposal repugnant in light of how Jesus lived and taught, that agenda item becomes licit and valid. Then the proposal goes to the Pope for validity as an item on the *Instrumentum Laboris* of the final Assembly of Bishops in 2024.

Pope Francis begins by calling the attention of the Curia to his criteria and asserts that the criteria constitute the foundational essence of Catholicism. Pope Francis thereby saves face for the Curia but dodges the key issue of the Curia, "Who has access, sole or otherwise, to the Holy Spirit?" Francis simplifies the proceedings of the Council. In effect, Pope Francis assigns the presence of the Holy Spirit to the Bishops in assembly.

The Curia has no argument: If a proposition does not contradict the ten commandments, the great commandment and the creed, and then upon examination by the Bishops, the proposition is seen as fitting in with what we know of Jesus from the gospel, The Curia has to agree that the Bishops are in possession of the Holy Spirit.

The proposals that survive the review by the Bishops then become part of the working paper prepared by Cardinal Grech, who presents the working paper for the Pope's approval. Next, the proposal is to be reviewed and voted up or down in the final 2024 Assembly.

In October 2024, the Bishops assembled in Council decide whether the proposal, upon a further review, falls within Pope Francis' common field. Upon the Bishops' re-evaluation, each proposal that makes sense within the life and teaching of Jesus still has one more test: How does it fit into the operation of the Church?

The Church Society has protocols and there needs to be a discussion and judgment about how that proposition will work within the Church organization. Some rather elaborate and current protocols may need a further crafting. For example, if the Catholic Church were to end up with female Cardinals, does the continuation of prestigious titles continue against the possibility of having "Princesses" of the Church?

## *Going Forward: Engage the World*

In his publication, *Catholicism,* noted Notre Dame University historian John T. McGreevy offers a major insight: going forward in the newly sophisticated world, the Church is going to be pressed because its old method of addressing the world[2] will be questioned and rejected. The Church will need new thinking. The Church will be required to make sense, talk intelligently about its positions, and relate to the science of the new times.

A preliminary survey of the work of current upcoming theologians reveals a foundation for a Church open to whatever the world presents. Areas to which today's theologians have been especially sensitive are those of medicine's biological systems and psychiatry's understanding of human motivation and needs. These relate especially to moral sexual behavior and norms. The world of the theologian has changed and no

---

[2] We are right and that is that!

longer relies on Latin syllogisms or citation from biblical texts, but instead has given way to citations from scientific journals. The Church scholars reach into the depths of modern science to refresh the presuppositions of the Church theology and morality.

An example of such an approach can be found in several *dubeats* published on the subject of the Church's moral theology of sexual conduct. The *dubeats* draw on the depth of medical and psychiatric knowledge that underpins the new and expanded understandings of the human person. How all the systems of the body integrate within and influence the human personality have been lacking in the underpinning of Catholic moral theology. Put crudely, one example is the Church can no longer treat the morality of serious married couples' intercourse as though it were a barnyard cattle coupling. The Church needs to rethink what it means to be a human person and how persons relate to one another in their totality of needs and affections.

Finally, we must not forget: the Holy Spirit has the back of Pope Francis in the Synodal Process. The Bishops meet to seek the Holy Spirit in their decision-making; they seek to find the full expression of Jesus in the lives of the Faithful. Will their deliberations show an appreciation of the *sensus fidelium*? What new verbalizations of inspirations from the Holy Spirit will emerge? Will the Paraclete, the Jesus promise, show along the way in the Assembly of Bishops? Pope, Bishops, and all pew-Catholics need pray the usual petition: "Come Holy Spirit, fill the hearts of your Faithful."

We always need to remember whatever the Vatican Battle of the Bishops produces:

## ECCLESIA SEMPER REFORMANDA

**"The Church is always in need of reformation...**

**In so far as she is an institution of men."**

**—The Bishops of the Council, Vatican II**

# APPENDIX:

## Is God Just Looking to be a Close Friend?
## Is That Why Jesus Came?

In this Appendix we return to the problem of Original Sin as an unverifiable event. It has a mythical base and accompanies a description of the Big Bang to which no person was or could have been a witness. Recalling the objections to the centrality and the cited problems with the doctrine of Original Sin, we take time to review what theologians have suggested or might suggest as an alternative central doctrine.

Medieval theologians seem to have been a playful lot. We remember some of the questions that were favorites for *disputanda*: "How many angels can stand on the head of a pin?" And the Zeno problem: "Can you cross a room if you have to go halfway?" Today, perhaps a theologian might speculate with a different kind of question like, "What does the Pope say to a person from outer space?" After all, some astrophysicists speculate that as soon as five years from now the Earth may be visited by intelligent beings from space. That is scary, not because we need to fear physical harm but rather because our visitors will expect that we are intelligent beings. We are expected to be able to think, to enjoy art and music, and to make sense of what we do and what we believe.

Picture this: St.Peter's Square, the Vatican, the year 2037. The television crews have just set up their gear and trained the cameras on the chairs where Pope Rome is about to grant an open-air audience to the Captain of Outer-Space Rocket 47, Commander Extraterra. After the usual ceremonial exchange of state-sponsored gifts, the sound of camera shutters subsides and an anticipatory silence creeps over the curious crowd of journalists and tourists.

The Pope and Commander engage in dialogue:

Extraterra: What is this you call religion? We are not familiar with your practice.

Pope Rome: Religion is an organized body of beliefs we hold and take very seriously. Those beliefs are codified to offer us humans an understanding of our meaning, why we are here on earth, and our purpose. Finally, from our purpose, we derive a prescription for proper human thinking and right human behavior.

E: Fascinating! May I ask what is the major thrust of your beliefs? Your core belief?

P: We believe that a being whom we call God is the Creator of our world. Further, our core belief then centers on God's son, Jesus, whom God sent to became one of us to redeem us from our sins; sins are our failures to live according to the prescriptive proper human thinking or right behavior.

E: That's absolutely fascinating! I'm especially curious about God sending his son to redeem you. Just how horribly did you humans sin to warrant God having to send his own son?

P: Well, it was not really something specific that we did. We do sin and we accept that we have a general tendency to sin. But to explain our tendency to sin, we follow a myth. The myth tells of God creating the universe and how the first person he created sinned by disobeying God. In the myth, that person is given the name of Adam. The belief system places Jesus, God's son, as the counterpoint to Adam; Jesus redeems us from Adam's sin, the symbol of all our sinning.

E: I want to make sure I understand. Let me get this straight: God sent his son to redeem you from a storybook man committing a storybook sin? Well, I suppose it's okay if you also have a storybook Jesus.

P: No, Jesus is a real person and lived a little over 2,000 years ago.

E: I'm sorry! I have a real problem with that! To me it seems that you imagine your god to be a fool. Why would a god, a god who's intelligent and smart enough and powerful enough to create this universe, send his son to die for a make-believe sin by a make-believe man?

P: First, please understand that in the realm of religion, we are dealing with symbols. There is no way that a human can comprehend God, and all the more, there is no way human language can express the spiritual reality that is unseen. Language becomes totally inadequate in talking about the non-material, the spiritual, and God. For now just hold this idea: religion must use symbolism because it is necessary.

You see, it all started when we humans did not know that the Adam story was a myth. An early zealot in our ranks by the name of Paul thought it was history. He elaborated the story to explain to his followers why he thought Jesus came to earth. After we learned the Bible was not history, we decided to leave things the way they were. If not literally true, the fact of the matter is that story, and the derived doctrine, carry the symbolic truth of man's tendency to sin and of man's need for redemption.

E: But you still teach that literally about your Jesus? People still accept those beliefs literally, or do they? I take it from your explanation that you haven't made your followers aware of the storybook character of their beliefs.

P: That's true. We have not approached them with a discussion of myth. We consider that it would confuse them; maybe cause them to regard their purpose and responsibilities in life less seriously than they should.

E: I'm sorry but I have a hard time with that. My trouble is respecting and accepting you and your organization. You command an organization that allows its members to base their very lives on a myth. You choose to live in a fuzzy, semi-fantasy world called symbolism. And you choose to insist on your followers doing the same. I'm suspicious of people like that. I want to work with people who are fully engaged with reality.

Abrupt end of audience and interview! Neither Pope Rome nor Commander Extraterra have paused for questions.

**Warnings from Theologians**

Church-recognized theologians have warned the Hierarchy of the weakness and the vulnerability associated with the Church's central doctrine; that Jesus came to atone for Adam's sin based on a myth is problematic. The doctrine of Jesus' sacrifice to overcome an Original Sin reaches into other doctrines and practices of the Church extensively. The Mass, attended by millions of worshipers every Sunday, is celebrated as the sacrifice of Jesus' atonement for sins in the Pauline tradition. The strict teaching on the Sacrament of Baptism stresses its absolute need for one's admission into heaven because of the scar of Original Sin. The Lenten season and services are centered around the role of a suffering Jesus because of the sin-and-redemption economy of Biblical sin.

During Vatican II and for a brief period afterward, theologians began to publish work which they had previously shelved. Before the "throw-open-the-windows" of Pope John XXIII, the Papal Curial Offices intimidated theologians. After Vatican II and its declaration of the legitimacy of independent thought and the responsibility of the individual conscience, many theologians dusted off their work. Sadly, after John XXIII, members of the Hierarchy (whose views were rejected at Vatican II) were elected popes. Pope John Paul II and Benedict XVI deliberately suppressed or actually excommunicated giant theological scholars whose research carried the relevancy of the Catholic Faith into the modern time: Cardinal Tissa Balasuryia, Karl Rahner, John Courtney Murray, Bernhard Haring, Rosemary Radford-Ruether, Richard McBrien, Yves Congar, and Charles Curran. Their "offense" was to counsel the Vatican to accept the realities of doctrine, its nature, and the authority it carries. Popes John Paul II and Benedict XVI ruled the Church without regard for the Bishops in the Council Vatican II. They insisted on the status quo because it was their familiar old Church; that is what they were comfortable in.

Two key doctrines with which theologians took issue were Original Sin and Apostolic Tradition. The theologians point out the doctrine of original sin is based on a myth, unverifiable, troubling to the modern mind, and taken too seriously by the Faithful. As to Apostolic Tradition, the Hierarchy claims its position of power on the basis of succession, in that the Bishop of Rome can be traced through history as successor to St. Peter. Apostolic Tradition cannot be verified, and the gospel passage relating Jesus' granting authority to Peter has textual problems. The text may be interpreted as guaranteeing constancy in truth to the entire body of Jesus believers.

Fr. Bernhard Haring was a Redemptorist-priest theologian. He pioneered the movement that took moral theology out of a listing of sins and the conditions that confirmed the commission of sin. Instead Fr. Haring placed human behavior against a foil of God's expectations of humans. He saw moral theology as what man could be, as a positive description of how children of God, in grateful response to the awe-inspiring love of their Maker, would seek to act according to God's plan and wishes.

On the basis of his research Fr. Haring, among many scholars, wondered about the weakness of the Church's foundation. Original Sin, the root of belief of the Church, relies on the unverifiable Genesis, then continues with St. Paul's interpretation of Jesus as the "second Adam." The vulnerability of the doctrine is Jesus as a savior to overcome a mythical sin of a mythical Adam.

Fr. Haring's reasoning goes like this: no one was present for the Big Bang. Therefore, the evidence for the doctrine of Original Sin is truly unverifiable. Genesis is a myth; a myth is not verifiable. What cannot be verified is not suitable and not foundational as the basis for the fundamental doctrine and mission of the Church.

Cardinal Tissa Balasuryia, Director of the Theology Department at the Sri Lanka Catholic University, has called attention to the human derivation of Church doctrine. He pointed to the nature and formation of theology. The Cardinal reminded the Church that theology is the work of the human mind. Theologians construct ideas about God, about our relation to God and to each other. The foundational doctrine of the

Church is that Adam's sin is our sin; fortunately for us it is corrected by the life and sacrifice of Jesus, but it is also a mental construct.

Cardinal Balasuryia is doubly motivated. First, he points to what is at stake—one of the implications of doctrine is to dictate the behavior of real people. Church members, threatened by mortal sin and excommunication for lack of belief, are put through needless grief and worry by unverifiable doctrine. Therefore, it is an absolute necessity the Church take into account the human consequences of its doctrine. It must be clear on its own merits. For that reason, Cardinal Balasuryia does not let go of the problems with the doctrine of Original Sin. The point of Balasuryia's argument is if the interpretation by Hebrew scholars, the original keepers of the Genesis story, do not hold that Original Sin belongs to anyone other than Adam, on what grounds can the Church Hierarchy justify its interpretation as applying to all of mankind? Thereby, he calls the attention of the Vatican to consider the Jewish Tradition that interprets the sin in Genesis as that of Adam alone.

Theologian Hans Küng, Emeritus Professor of Theology, University of Tubingen, served as *peritus*, an expert advisor to Vatican Council II appointed by Pope John XXIII. Fr. Küng was more prominent than other theologians because he was also a professorial colleague of Joseph Ratzinger, later Pope Benedict XVI.[3]

In 1971, Fr. Küng published his scholarly research, *Infallible? An Inquiry*.[4] Küng's book was well received and its arguments almost

---

[3] An irony lay in the Küng-Ratzinger relationship. Fr. Küng was Chairman of the Theology School at the University of Tubingen. He recommended then Fr. Ratzinger for a professorship there. Küng, later in his life, was censured for his theological writings by Ratzinger, who headed the Congregation for the Faith.

[4] The label "inquiry" because it is the English equivalent of the Latin *dubeat*.

universally reviewed and debated: there is no independent verification of the succession process as claimed by the Vatican. The succession in its substance is also under scrutiny as to whom the text applies, to Peter as leader of the apostles or to the entire body of Jesus followers. Nine years after its publication, the Vatican, in the person of Cardinal Ratzinger, called Fr. Küng to account for his thesis. After a rather superficial process and what appeared as a predetermined judgment, the Congregation for the Preservation of the Faith in the person of Ratzinger no longer declared Fr. Küng a Catholic Theologian.

Fr. Küng's work joins the work of other theologians who have been censured or otherwise disqualified as Catholic theologians. His work is an example of the Hierarchy's rejection of any change to the thinking of the status quo. There are to be no challenges to any doctrine; what the Magisterium holds is all truth. It appears no one is to evaluate any of the past against the theology of the present. Fr. Küng continued in his loyalty to the Church, but not as an official Catholic theologian; he continued his teaching at the Swiss University of Tubingen.

**Final Note on Original Sin**

Until St. Augustine chimed in, there was no universal concern about or understanding of the existence of Original Sin. In fact, two early Fathers of the Church, Gregory of Nazianzus and John Chrysostom, taught unbaptized children were without sin. Another, Pelagius, considered what Adam and Eve did pertained to them alone as individuals. Sometimes what the Iron Chancellor, Otto Von Bismarck, said applies to the Church: "It is good that the commoners do not know how sausage and laws [doctrine] are made."

## Jesus: A Special Sacrament of God

Jesus is the Sacrament of God, the person by whom the unclean world around us becomes the Kingdom of God. Jesus is central to "sacramentizing" the world. The mission of the Church is to rework the unclean world, make sure it becomes the Kingdom. Therefore, Jesus is to be—or should be—the central focus of the Catholic Church. Jesus is to be somehow the central doctrine of the Church. Early followers of Jesus remembered him as a rabbi who brought God down into their world, a sacrament, an outward sign of the invisible hand of God. How might the Church recreate that today?

Presently the Nicaean Creed defines the Catholic but what the folks saw in Jesus was someone who stood for something. What people stand for are values. Let's do a mental experiment: describe your dad or your mom. Heavy odds say you described them in terms of what was important to them. Those are values. To recreate what Jesus meant to the early followers, we might adopt a creed of values to recite each Sunday. "I believe in honoring my Creator; I believe in the sanctity of every person; I believe I am no better than the next person; I believe in honoring my family and neighbors; I believe in helping around the house; I believe in the unity of our Parish; I believe in honest dealings; I believe in helping others; I believe in..." Perhaps each parish might write its own special value-beliefs and keep them current by a rewrite each year. A post-Sunday-Mass meeting might be held to solicit what the pews want mentioned as a value-belief. The idea is to make the presence of Jesus the focus of the Church.

Jesus was the early followers' Sacrament of God. They intuited and experienced Jesus as the one who brings God into their lives. They then made Jesus central in their lives, conducting memorial meals, forming a society centered around their memories of Jesus. They made Jesus their doctrine: how he conducted himself, what he said, his stories, his pattern of dining, and his love shown in caring and healing.

The Catholic Church, if it were to acknowledge the need for a new central doctrine, has a model to follow in the devotion and practices of Jesus' early followers. Allow Jesus to become the central doctrine—to be our Special Sacrament of God. He began the work of sacramentizing the world; he was limited in space and time; he passed the task on to those who have ears to hear; he waits for the ultimate realization of the Kingdom of God at the end time.

Practically, the rules would be forgotten. Instead, the pulpit would tell of God's great love waiting to be requited, and remind folks of all the daily possibilities to requite God's love. For example, help someone get a job; remind spouses to seek the good for one another; caution parents that the Church school is not a substitute for their loving care and moral instruction of the children; encourage those in the marketplace to do fair deals, to succeed; maintain secure employment for their workers; keep tabs on quality to assure a reasonably working product; and maintain a steady dividend flow to the shareholders. Also, remind those who succeeded economically about ways they might requite God's love by addressing needs in the parish or larger society. Finally, remind everyone the Church is an institution of us humans, welcoming the broken, the sad, and the sinner just as Jesus did.

**Would God Still Have Come If We Had Not Sinned?**

The idea of modifying the Church's central doctrine is not new. Recall the philosophers and theologians at the height of Scholasticism were a playful lot. Even on the question of what happens if we change the central doctrine of the Church, some theologians had asked that question back then. In the Eleventh Century, an English Benedictine theologian and scholar, Rupert of Deutz, became curious enough to ask the question about whether God still would have become man if humans had not sinned. In addition to Rupert came theologians interested in that same question: in the Twelfth Century, Franciscan Duns Scotus and Dominican Albert the Great; in the Thirteenth Century, theologian Franciscan Alexander of Hakles. These old-timers and the modern theologians answer with a "Yes." They are convinced God's love for us would have impelled God to join us. Paraphrasing scripture: God so loved the world that he joined his children in their humanity.

In the December 15, 2022 issue of the *National Catholic Rep*orter, theologian Fr. Daniel P. Horan wrote an article titled, "What Is The Real Reason for the Season: Sin Or Love?" Horan offers a sketch of the theologians who wondered: "If Original Sin was why Jesus came to earth, would God have become man if we humans had not sinned?" That's certainly a good Medieval question; ranks much higher in import than all those angels standing on the head of a pin. Horan's point is that every theologian agreed that God's love for us would have caused God to become a man alongside us.

To wrap up his article, Fr. Daniel Horan refers us to Trappist Father Thomas Merton's *New Seeds Of Contemplation*. There Fr. Merton's conclusion is God loves us so much that God wants to be with and right alongside us. Merton suggests God's love for us is so deep and so intense that it won't allow God simply to have us adore him; his love demands a closeness, very personal and intimate, tighter (and more) than we have with our closest friends. God's love can't stand the idea that we shrink away from God as all-powerful, that we keep a remote, somewhat fearful relationship; God does not want a cold and formal friendship, like a starched hospital bed sheet. God wants us to know him, up close and warm, to hang with him as we do with our regular gang. With that observation about God's craving for a close friendship with us, Fr. Daniel Horan is able to conclude with a jubilant exultation about Christmas: God's love! That's the reason for the season!

## Conclusion

The pew-Catholic has a three-pronged option for belief in Jesus: First, Jesus is our Savior who saves us from the consequences of the mythical sin of the mythical Adam, symbolizing our sinful tendencies. Second, Jesus is a Special Sacrament of God who shows us how to sanctify the unclean world for the Father. Finally, Jesus is our Special Friend who brings his formal God-ship into a close, casual but deeply warm and intimate heart-to-heart loving friendship with each of us. The beauty of the triple option is that none of them is exclusive of the others. We may, perhaps guided by the liturgical season or our sense of devotion, hold all of the options the theologians have thought to present to us.

To think of God and Jesus in oddball ways can and has been rewarding. Fr. Daniel Horan gave us a new way to think about Jesus at Christmas. An English essayist also thought of Jesus in an unusual way.

G. K. Chesterton called attention to the fact that one of the best and most welcome attributes of a human person is a sense of humor. He went on to observe a sense of humor is not anywhere reported of Jesus in the gospels. Chesterton concluded with his tongue in his cheek: Jesus' God-sense of humor is so great that he dare not show it because we'd all literally die laughing.

On the serious side, Fr. Rahner described Jesus as God's perfect expression of His God-ness in a human person. Jesus wants to be our closest friend, and Jesus awaits our R.S.V.P.

# AUTHOR BIOGRAPHY

Gil Gadzikowski retired as Chairman of the Board, President, and Chief Executive Officer of First National Bank in Sioux City and First Federal Savings & Loan of Council Bluffs, Iowa.

As a young man, Gil joined the Jesuits in the hope of a presumed vocation to the priesthood. That was not to be, and after eight years of Jesuit study and training, Gil entered the business world as an IBM Service Bureau salesman. That was followed by middle management and executive positions in insurance and banking. Prior to assuming his Chief Executive Officer positions in banking, Gil was Senior Bank Consultant with the Chicago firm of Lester B. Knight & Associates and its European partner Knight-Wiegenstein in Zurich. He served clients in the United States, Italy, Belgium, and the United Kingdom.

Gil devoted his retirement time and energy to the study and analysis of religion and specifically the Catholic Church. From that research comes *The Vatican Battle of Bishops: A View from the Pew.* Immersed in the work of the Bishops of Vatican II, Gil concentrated on the programmatic features of the decrees and especially on the contribution of John Courtney Murray, S.J. The empowerment of the Faithful by the Holy Spirit, the failure of the Hierarchy to act on priestly sexual abuse, their attempt at a cover-up, and Pope Francis' calling forth the Holy Spirit from the pews all motivated this self-publication of his retirement research into the Catholic Church.

Gil earned the Bachelor of Arts in Philosophy and Economics and Rome's Gregorian Degree of Licentiate in Philosophy at St. Louis University; at Marquette University, the Master of Arts in Economics. Gil served as Instructor in Latin and Greek, Campion Jesuit High

School; Instructor in Economics, Benedictine University; and Visiting Professor in Finance and Management, Creighton University, Heider Business School.

Gil relishes the license of retirement to stay up way past midnight delving into the thoughts of others, reliving the passage of historic times, or frustrating over an entry in a crossword puzzle—conscious of the snuggly pleasure of sleeping in the next morning. Family and friends are embraced by favored home visits, dawdling over lazy lunches and engaging the convenience of today's electronic mail. A would-have-been athlete, Gil follows Marquette and Creighton in Big East basketball; and in football favors Notre Dame and Green Bay.

Milton Keynes UK
Ingram Content Group UK Ltd.
UKHW020734190124
436321UK00014B/629

9 781647 198794